Santa Showcase

WOODCARVING ILLUSTRATED

Alan Giagnocavo
Publisher

Peg Couch
Acquisition Editor

Shannon Flowers
Editor

Troy Thorne
Creative Direction

Jon Deck
Layout

ISBN 978-1-56523-340-9

Santa showcase / [by the editors of] Woodcarving illustrated. -- East Petersburg, PA : Fox Chapel Publishing, c2007.

p. ; cm.
ISBN: 978-1-56523-340-9
1. Wood-carving--Patterns. 2. Wood-carved figurines--Patterns.
3. Christmas decorations--Patterns. 4. Santa Claus.
I. Woodcarving illustrated.

TT200 .S26 2007
745.594/12--dc22 0711

Printed in China
10 9 8 7 6 5 4 3 2 1

Woodcarving Illustrated • 1970 Broad Street, East Petersburg, PA 17520

www.woodcarvingillustrated.com

Contents

Celebrating 10 Years of Santa Carving

When *Woodcarving Illustrated* published its very first issue back in September 1997, we were cautiously optimistic. We only printed one third of the copies that we print today, and sold out of back issues within six months. A copy of the first issue is a recurring request from our customers.

That first printing is the physical manifestation of my dream: A dream to share the talents of skilled artists with novice carvers, a dream to showcase the beauty of carved wood and to promote the craft to new generations.

Ten years later, we're still following that dream. Every issue of *Woodcarving Illustrated* features skilled craftsmen who enthusiastically share their talents and highlights some of today's best carvers. It's with great pride that I present this showcase of the best Santa patterns collected from 10 years of publishing the premiere magazine for woodcarvers.

Alan Giagnocavo

Publisher

The History of Santa

NICHOLAS, THE BISHOP OF MYRA, is commonly credited as the inspiration for the modern day Santa Claus. Orphaned at a young age, Nicholas devoted his life to the Christian Church. The earliest documentation of his generous acts occurred in the third century AD. At this time, it was still customary for fathers to offer a dowry for their daughters to their prospective husbands. According to legend, one man was too poor to offer a dowry for his three daughters, who, without a husband, would be sold into slavery. Mysteriously, a bag of gold was thrown down the chimney on three separate occasions. According to the legend, the gold fell into stockings that were hanging near the fire to dry and so the custom of children hanging their stockings by the hearth on Christmas began.

There are several other stories of how Nicholas helped children, which eventually led to him being named a saint by the church. To this day, he is venerated as the patron saint of children. Most Olde World-style Santa carvings, which tend to depict Santa in flowing, vaguely ecclesiastical robes, are based on Saint Nicholas.

Over time, the tradition spread across Europe, and most Catholics celebrated the feast of St. Nicholas on December 6, which is still the main gift-giving day in Europe.

As the Protestants broke away from the Catholic Church, they tried to stop celebrating the festivals associated with St. Nicholas. But the common people loved St. Nick, and it was difficult to stamp out the celebrations.

Since many of the first settlers to the United States were Protestants, the gift-giving traditions of Christmas were not as common. But there were still some regions that kept up the traditions. The German immigrants in Pennsylvania celebrated the feast of St. Nicholas, and there are accounts of St. Nicholas visiting the Dutch in New York.

Santa, circa 1895.

***Bishop of Myra*, the patron saint of children, sailors, and animals. Carved by Art Shoemaker.**

The jolly elf image for St. Nicholas, which the Dutch called Sinterklaas, or Santa Claus, got a boost in 1823 when the poem, "A Visit from St. Nicholas" was written. This poem, which is also known as "The Night Before Christmas," became popular and provided a detailed description of Santa Claus and his sleigh pulled by eight reindeer. The ninth, Rudolph, was introduced in 1939 by the Montgomery Ward company.

The most popular image of Santa Claus was drawn by Thomas Nast, a political cartoonist for *Harper's Weekly*. This drawing was loosely based on the popular poem and several other descriptions of the holiday figure. Nast also came up with the concept of Santa's workshop being populated by elves.

Nast's drawing, while black and white, could be considered the inspiration for the classic Coca Cola Santa, the bearded fellow dressed all in red. This Santa was unveiled in a series of advertisements in 1931.

'Twas the Night Before Christmas, circa 1898.

Santa Claus, drawn by Thomas Nast of *Harper's Weekly*.

Santa Claus in Camp, *Harper's Weekly*, circa 1863.

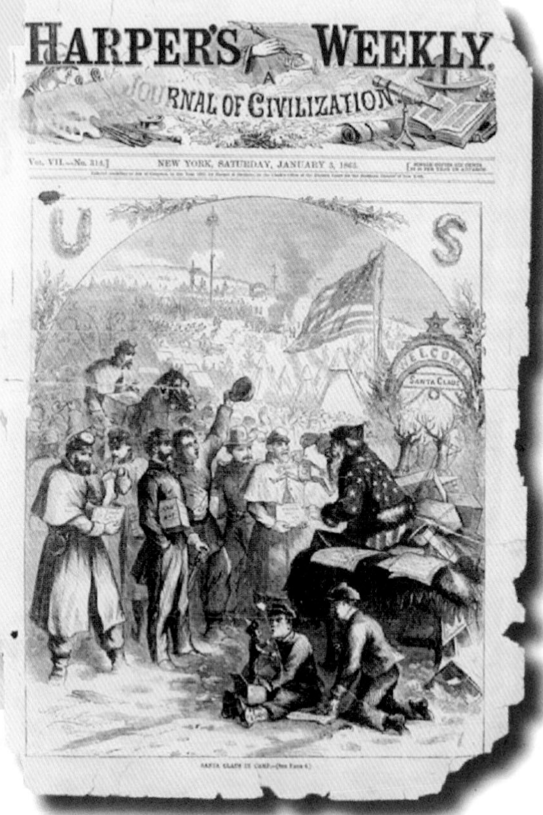

HARPER'S WEEKLY.
A JOURNAL OF CIVILIZATION

Vol. VII.—No. 314.] NEW YORK, SATURDAY, JANUARY 3, 1863.

Santa is not the only mythical figure inspired by St. Nicholas. German children put a boot, called Nikolaus-Stiefel, outside their doors for St. Nicholas to fill with candy and small toys. In the United Kingdom, Father Christmas leaves something under the tree for the children. Scandinavian children send letters to Jultomten, who delivers toys in a sleigh pulled by goats. In the Netherlands, Sinterklaas dons a red bishop's dress and brings gifts to every child that has been good in the past year. French children receive presents from Père Noël.

Not every Christmas gift giver is based on St. Nicholas, though. In Italy, a kindly witch called La Befana flies down chimneys to leave presents for children. In Russia, Babouschka, an elderly lady, knowingly gave the Wise Men the wrong directions, and later felt remorse. Now she leaves presents for all the children, hoping that one will be the infant Jesus, and she will be forgiven.

No matter what form he takes, or where the inspiration comes from, the figure associated with Christmas and gift giving is most often based on the qualities of generosity and selflessness. The physical appearance is open to interpretation by the individual artist, but the spirit of Santa Claus harkens back to the Bishop of Myra, who put the needs of others before his own.

Père Noël, the French Father of Christmas. Carved by Art Shoemaker.

La Befana, the lady gift giver of Italy. Carved by Art Shoemaker.

Saint Nicholas with Noah's Ark. **Carved by Art Shoemaker.**

Saint Nickolas, **6" high. Carved in butternut by Mark & Janet Klein.***

Saint Nickolas **bust in basswood. Carved and painted by Mark & Janet Klein.***

* photos courtesy Reasons to Believe
http://reasonstobelieve.com

Christkindle, meaning Christ Child, was a replacement for Saint Nicholas during the Reformation. Carved by Art Shoemaker.

Saint Nicholas, Protector of Animals. Carved by Art Shoemaker.

Weihnachtsmann, **the old Christmas man of Germany. Carved by Art Shoemaker.**

Christmas Man, **basswood. Carved and painted by Vaughn & Stephanie Rawson.***

Visit from Saint Nick, **basswood. Carved and painted by Vaughn & Stephanie Rawson.***

Father Christmas, Great Britain's version of Saint Nicholas. Carved by Art Shoemaker.

Victorian Kris Kringle, inspired by an antique postcard. Carved by Art Shoemaker.

Norwegian Julesvan features a coat and hat decorated in the traditional Norwegian style. Carved by Art Shoemaker.

Scandinavian Santa, holding the traditional Dalecarlian horse. Carved by Barbara Scoles.*

Santa's Aviary depicts Santa making his rounds to feed his feathered friends. Carved by Barbara Scoles.*

Imperial Red Santa, carved from linden. Traditional Russian Santa painted in rich reds with gold trim.*

St. Nikita was the patron saint of Moscow and Russia. Carved by Art Shoemaker.

Russian Santa 'n Owl carved from linden with beautifully painted details.*

Painting Santa

by Michele Carville-Stetson

This two-foot-tall Santa, carved by Dave Stetson, is the perfect medium for demonstrating painting techniques like side loading, shading and highlighting. Inexpensive craft colors are used without confusing mixing formulas.

As a teacher of Santa carving and painting, I encourage my students to use craft paints made by Americana and Delta Ceramcoat. They are relatively inexpensive, consistent in texture and color, and reduce the worry in already anxious woodcarvers when it comes to painting.

Before sharing my "secrets," I have to admit that I used to paint my Santas with heavy, intense reds so the wood grain wouldn't show. Santa collectors, I reasoned, did not want the figures done with washes that made the colors look faded. In the hopes of providing my jolly St. Nicks with shading and depth of color, I would "antique" them with various concoctions of noxious smelling oil paints and a variety of mediums. The look satisfied the collectors for awhile. But several years ago, potential customers started asking why my "castings" were so expensive. When I indignantly informed them these figures were original woodcarvings, not reproductions, the would-be buyers told me that they really couldn't tell the difference.

I had to agree with their criticisms. There was no way to know whether the figure was wood or resin without cutting away some of the paint. So the search began for a more effective approach to impart rich colors to the carvings while allowing the wood grain to project through. Needless to say, there were many ruined Santas as I searched for the right paints and techniques. But as luck and persistence would have it, and with a little help from my partner, Dave Stetson, I came upon a system that works.

Acrylic Paint Washes

Heavy applications of colors are not the answer. Layering paint is, and that requires practice and patience. Practice is needed not only for the actual painting process, but also for knowing how much water to combine with the paints. Acrylic paints are not made to be mixed with water. Instead, they are designed to be cleaned up with water. When you add a drop of acrylic paint to a predetermined amount of water, and mix the two, the paint pigment usually ends up in the bottom of the cup. The process makes it impossible to lay on consistent, even color. If you have ever had your paint look granule-like, you will immediately understand. Ideally, acrylic paints should be combined with a flow medium, glaze or extender. However, most of these mediums delay the drying process. My approach is to use water as a thinner, but I add it to the brush first and then go to the paint.

Loading the Brush

To ensure an even application of paint, first dip the tips of the bristles in water and allow the water to wick up to the ferrule. Gently touch the tip of the brush on a dry paper towel to remove any potential water drips; then pull a small amount of paint from your palette with the brush. Mix the color up into the brush with a back and forth motion. Don't be afraid to put some pressure on the brush to allow the bristles to separate. When individual brush hairs collect paint, the brush is evenly loaded. When the water in the brush has blended with the paint, and the color is still intense, but you can see through it, it is ready to be applied to the carving.

As you run out of water, the bristles start to separate, so repeat the process of filling your brush by dipping the tips of the bristles in the water. Then, tap them off on a paper towel. Finally, pull paint from the puddle and blend on the palette. You won't need to wash out your brush until you change colors, unless the paint starts to dry on the brush. However, if you keep your brush saturated with enough water that should not happen.

Painting Techniques

There are three terms you need to be familiar with for my style of painting. These terms have been used by decorative painters for centuries, but they are just as applicable to woodcarving. Some may take getting used to, but the results will be impressive.

Side loading is a technique that requires filling the brush with water, lightly tapping off excess water on a paper towel to eliminate drips, and then running one side of the brush through the edge of the paint puddle so it picks up paint on that side. Then the brush is moved back and forth, not scrubbed side to side, on the palette so the paint works up in the brush while being lightly distributed across the brush. Make sure to keep the brush in the same track or paint stripe each time you move it back and forth. If you do this, the paint does not get spread all over the paper palette, which will cause you to run out of color prematurely. When the brush is properly loaded, you should be able to paint a swath of color that is intense on one side, but fading out to no color on the other. Practice side loading on the paper palette. If you end up with a heavy swath with no variation in color, wash out the brush and start over. This takes a little practice to master, but the effects you will achieve are worth the effort.

Shading means deepening shadows. This technique is useful for areas such as the folds, wrinkles and creases of clothing on a carving. To accomplish shading, a color darker than the basecoat is needed.

Highlighting requires using a lighter color than the basecoat to accentuate an area where a real or imaginary light source hits. The goal is to create a "higher" light, suggesting that the light source strikes this area first.

Brush Tips

Unless otherwise noted, I recommend a ½" oval shader for most of the Santa painting. Always use the largest brush possible to ensure even paint distribution. Too much time spent with an undersized brush and your chances of successfully applying an even coat of paint are diminished to almost zero. When using any brush, hold the handle perpendicular to the painted surface. This allows the paint to flow off the bristles with the help of gravity.

The brushes I prefer are made of taklon, a synthetic recommended for acrylic paints and watercolors. They are made by any number of brush companies and generally run in the $4 to $12 range. I advise you not to use expensive sable brushes on your woodcarvings. Most are too fragile to withstand the abuse that occurs when bristles come in contact with carvings.

materials & tools

PAINTS:

AMERICANA: Black Green, Cherry Red, Black Plum, Primary Yellow, Blush Flesh

DELTA CERAMCOAT: Adobe Red, Midnight Blue, Antique White, Salem Blue, Burnt Sienna, Timberline Green, Tomato Spice, Charcoal

JO SONJA: Rich Gold

MATERIALS:

Paper towels

Paper palette

1" disposable foam brush

Brushes: ½" oval shader, #3 round, 00 Script liner

Boiled linseed oil

Rust-Oleum American Accent clear matte finish

Water container

STEP BY STEP

Santa and Rudolph

by David Sabol
photography by Roger Schroeder

This charming Santa was featured on the cover of the premiere issue of *Woodcarving Illustrated*. Now sold out, that first issue has become a collector's item. We're pleased to share this timeless project with you as we celebrate *WCI*'s 10th anniversary.

David Sabol's Santa is carved from pine. He uses Minwax natural oil stain as a base and mixes in oil paints to achieve the vivid colors.

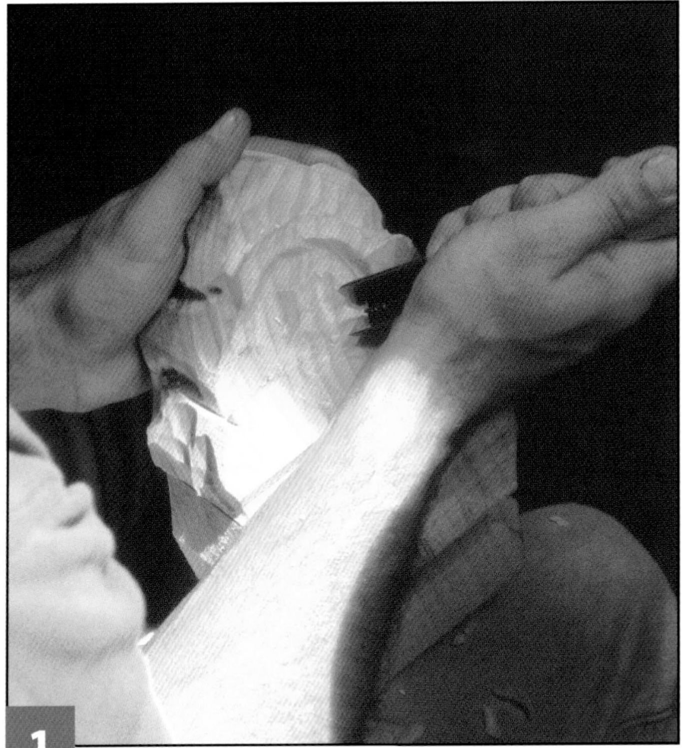

1 **Rough out the carving.** Cut the two profiles on a band saw. Use a large U-gouge, such as a 20mm #11 gouge, to break the carving down into the major areas. Choke up on the gouge and make shearing cuts to maintain control.

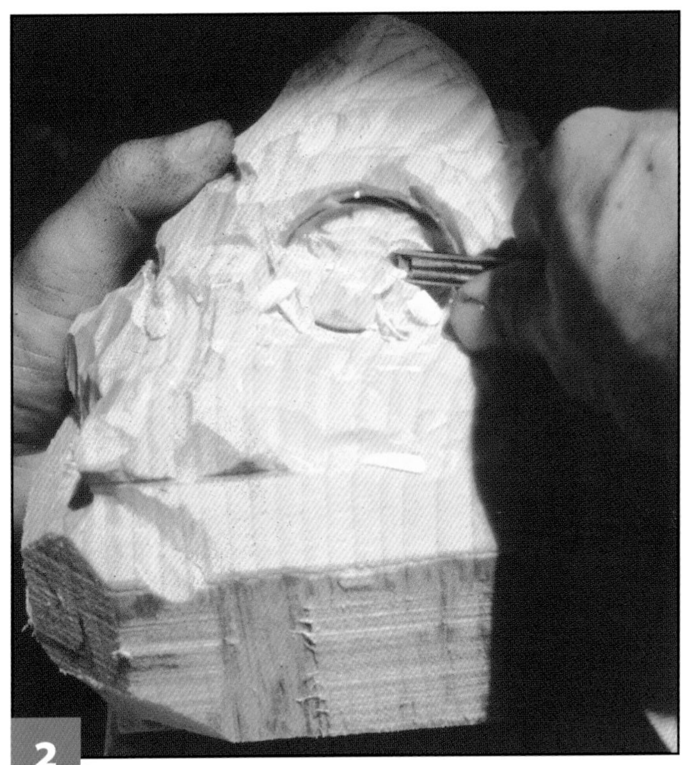

2 **Separate the hood from the face.** Use a small, deep gouge, such as a 7mm #9 gouge, to remove wood from the forehead and sides of the face so the hood protrudes. Block out the face and rough in the nose and cheeks.

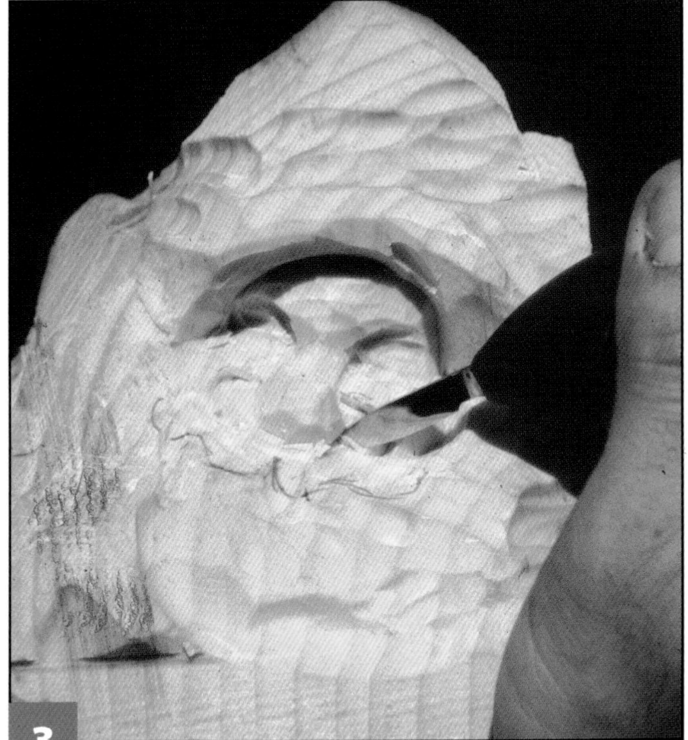

3 **Define the eyes and nose.** Use your carving knife of choice. I prefer a knife with a relatively stiff blade for this part of the carving. The blade needs to be long enough to get into the deep area, and a sturdy blade provides more control.

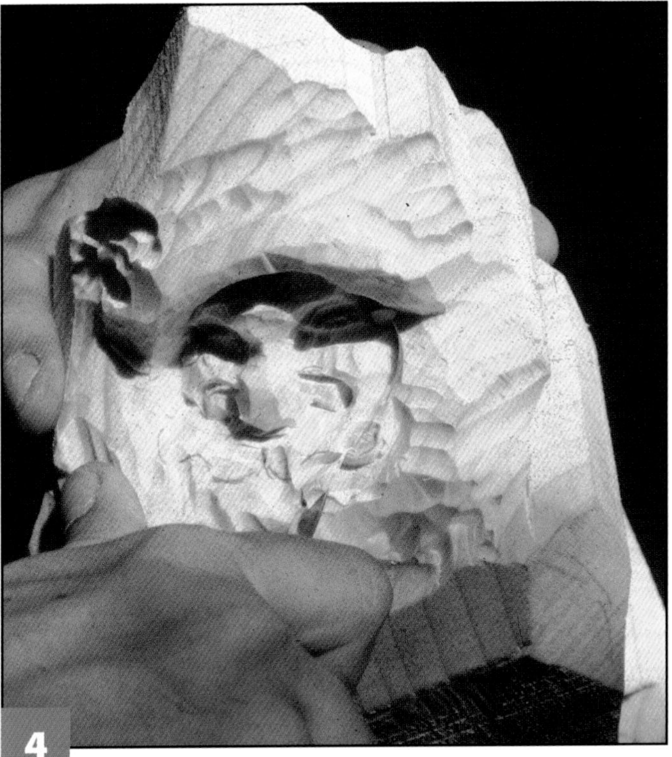

4 **Separate the moustache from the mouth and beard.** Use the same knife. I keep three points of contact with the carving at all times: holding it in my left hand, bracing the thumb of my right hand on the carving, and carving with the knife.

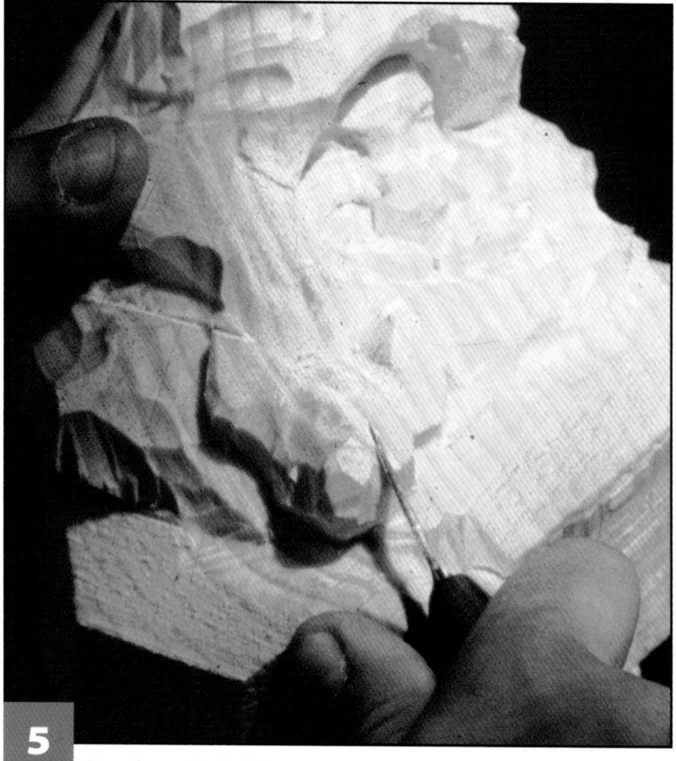

5 **Rough out Rudolph.** Since the baby reindeer is cradled in Santa's arms, this step consists of carving the basic shape of the head to use as a landmark.

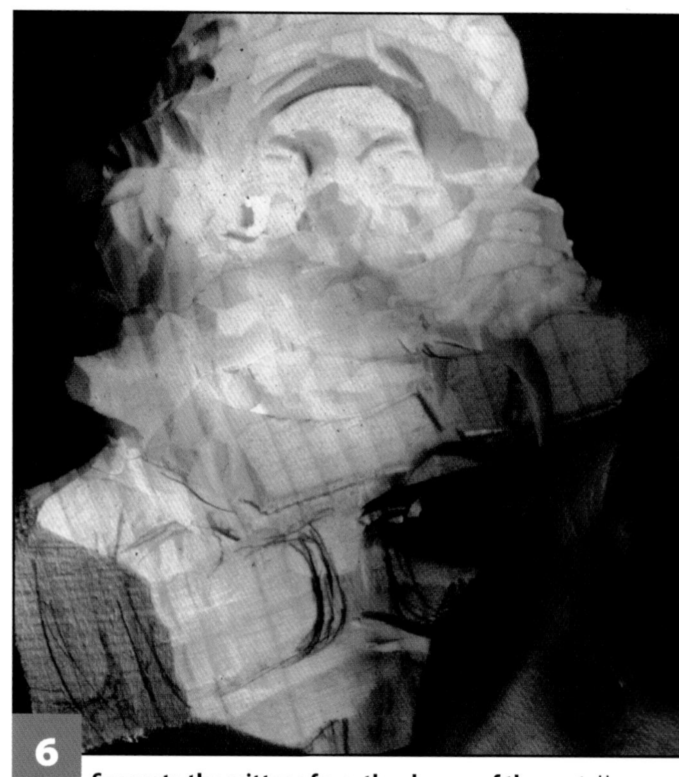

6 **Separate the mittens from the sleeves of the coat.** Use a small V-tool, such as a 45° 6mm V-tool, to outline the mittens. Remove wood from around the mittens to begin shaping the belly.

7 **Remove the wood between the mittens and the face.** Use a large U-gouge. Taper the mittens down about $^{3}/_{16}$" and relieve the wood around Rudolph's head to make it stand out.

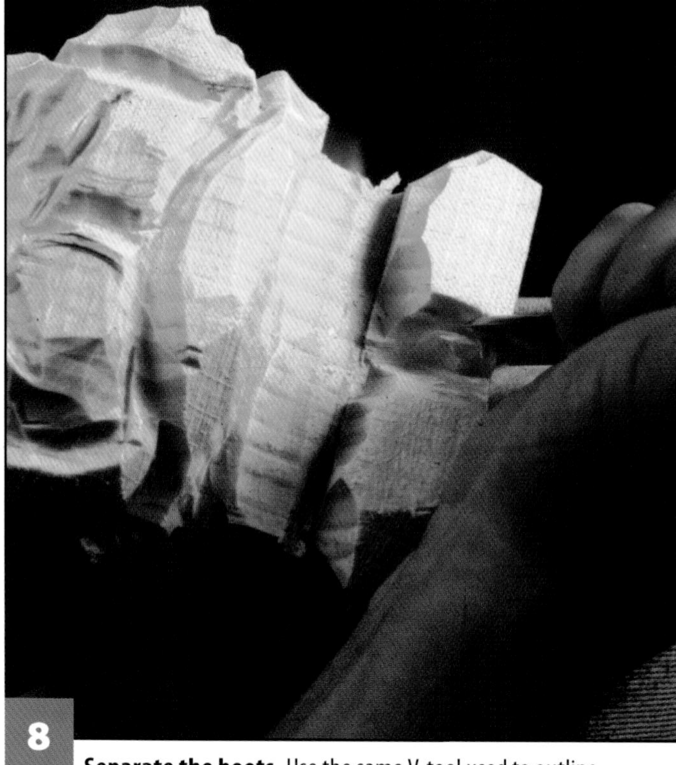

8 **Separate the boots.** Use the same V-tool used to outline the mittens. I move around on the carving often to maintain perspective and symmetry.

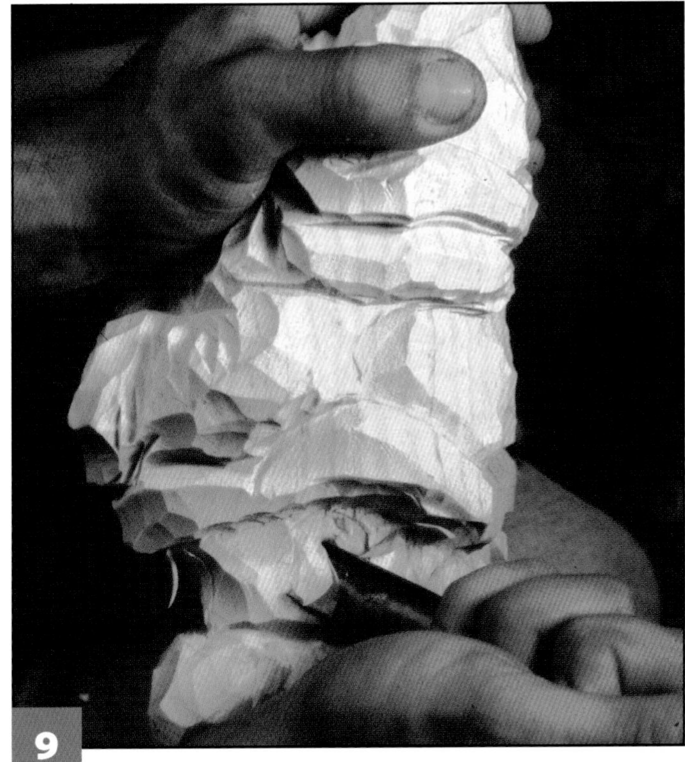

9 **Round the pant legs.** Use a large, medium-sweep gouge, such as a 18mm #7 gouge.

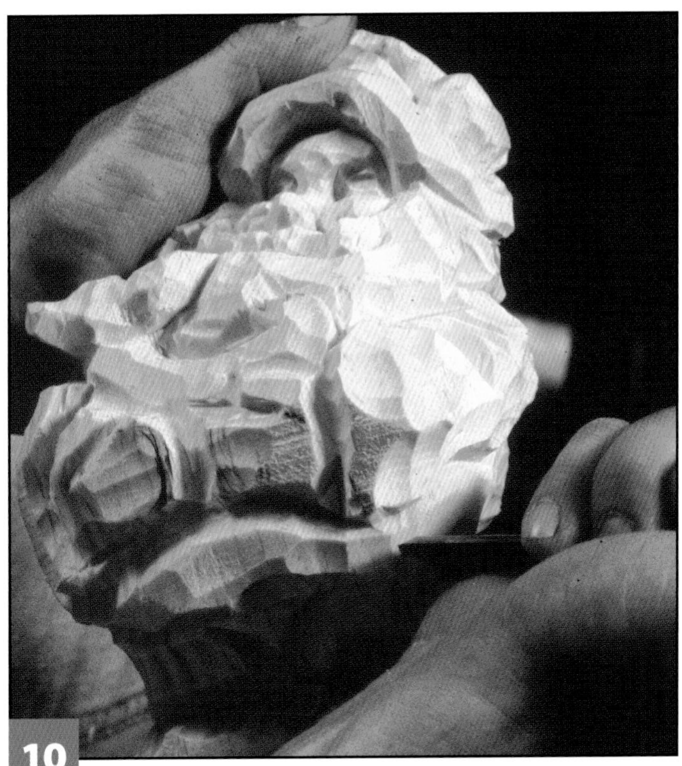

10 **Separate the coat fringe from the legs.** Use a large U-gouge.

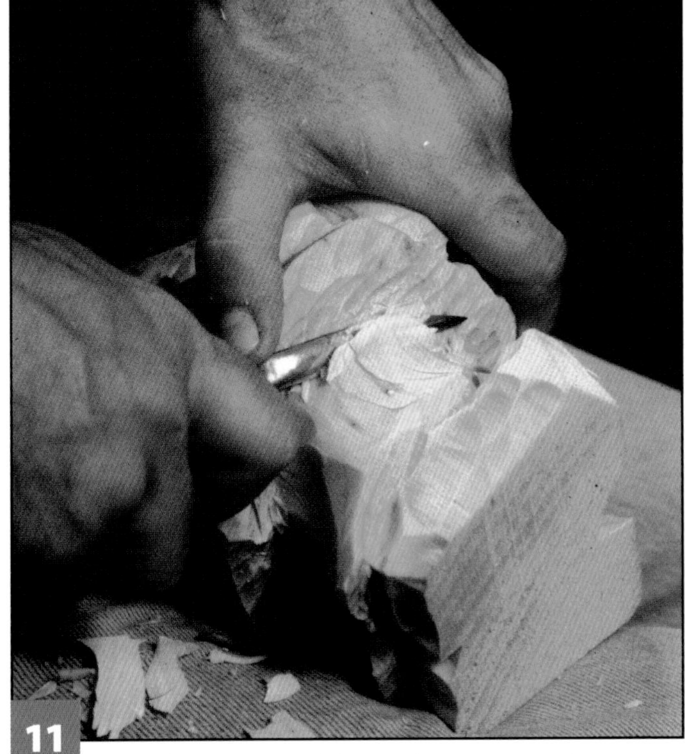

11 **Shape the area under the coat fringe.** For this, and any other tight areas, use a carving knife.

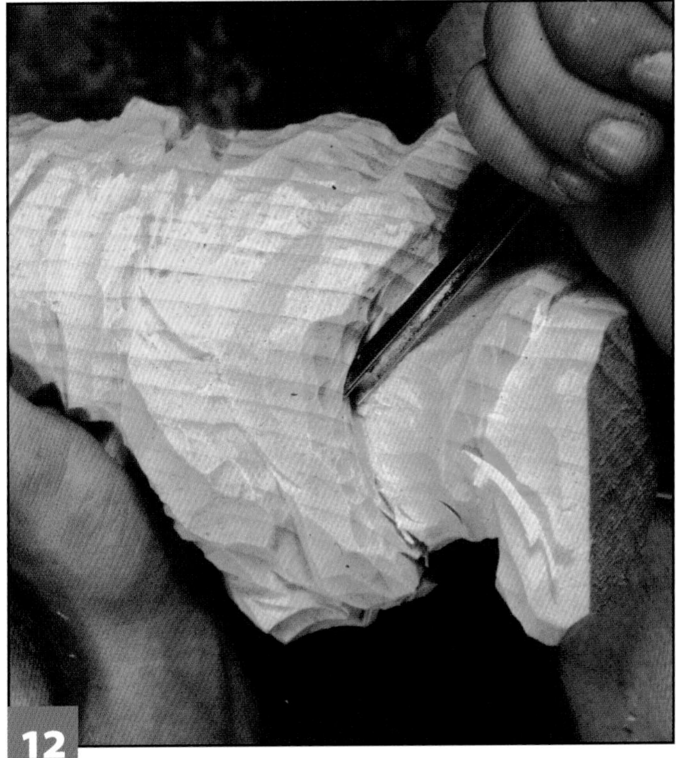

12 **Undercut the jacket.** Use the same V-tool used to separate the boots.

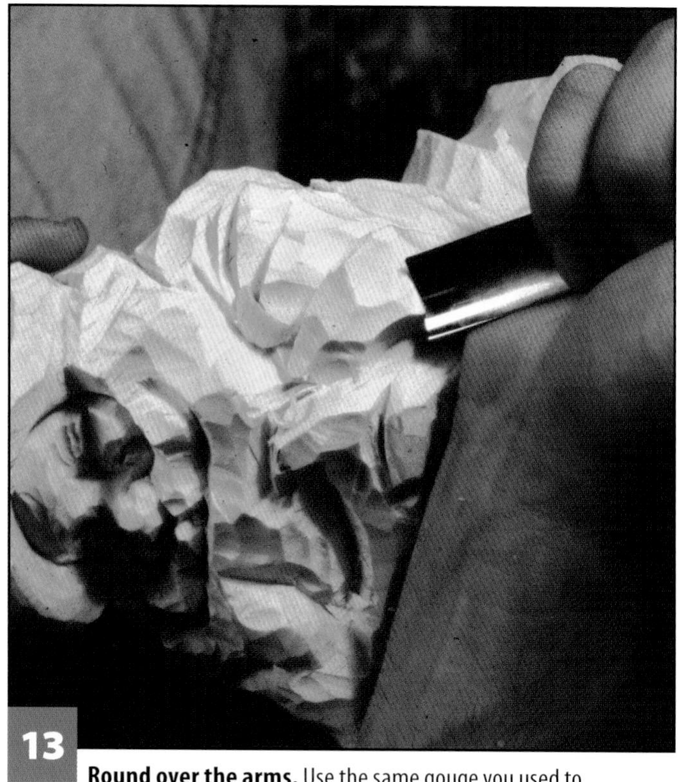

13 **Round over the arms.** Use the same gouge you used to round the legs.

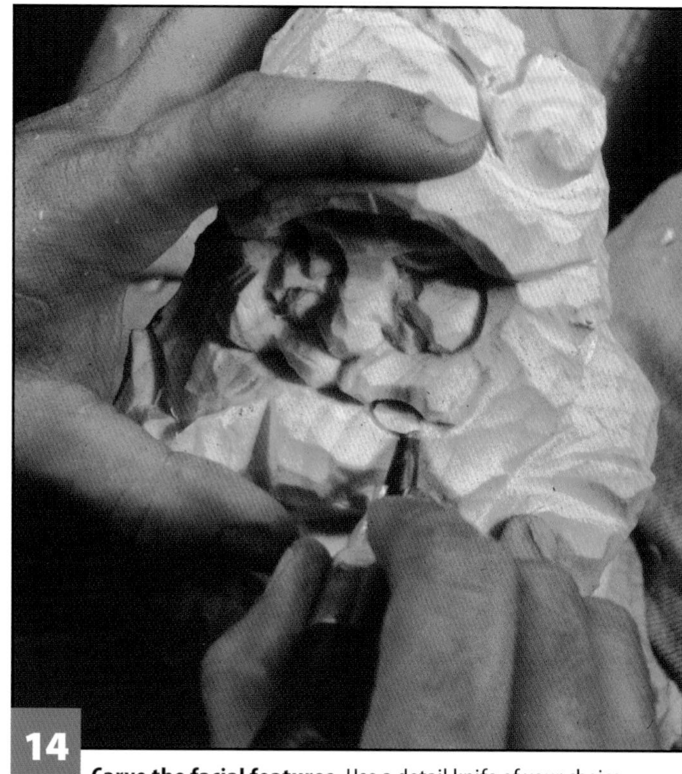

14 **Carve the facial features.** Use a detail knife of your choice. Make deep cuts to create shadows and add character.

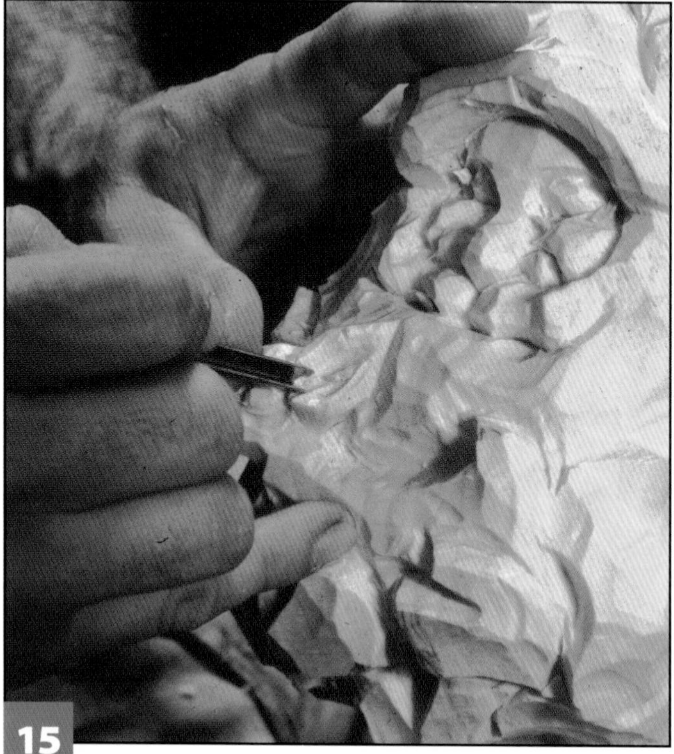

15 **Carve Rudolph to his final shape.** Use the pattern as a guide. Use a small U-gouge, such as a 4mm #11, to shape the inside of his ears.

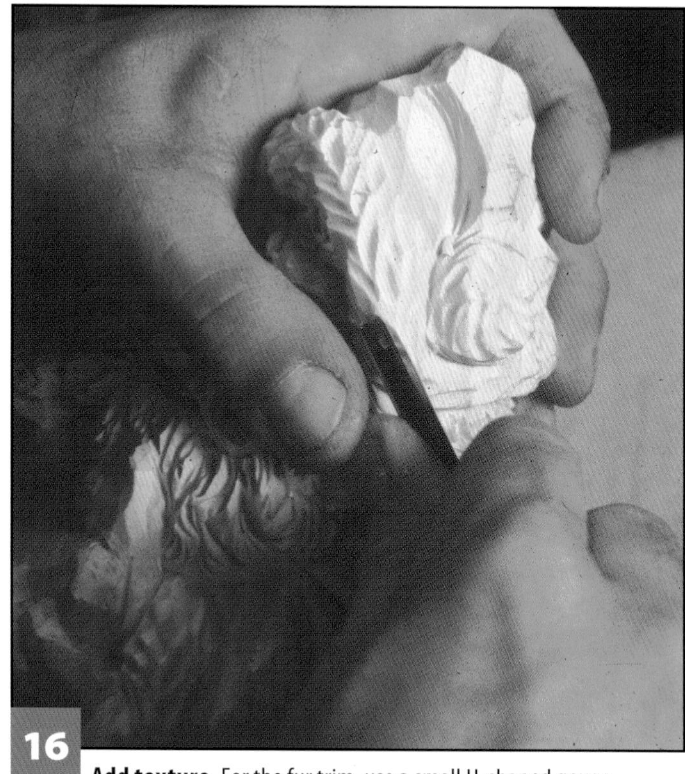

16 **Add texture.** For the fur trim, use a small U-shaped gouge, alternating the direction of the cuts. Switch to a small V-tool, such as a 45° 3mm V-tool, to texture the hair, beard, and moustache.

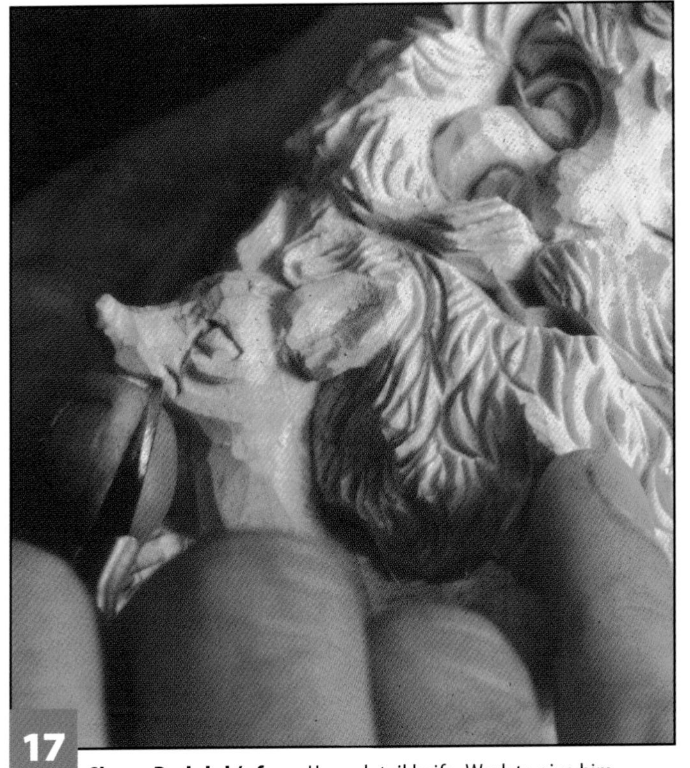

17 **Shape Rudolph's face.** Use a detail knife. Work to give him what looks like a smile.

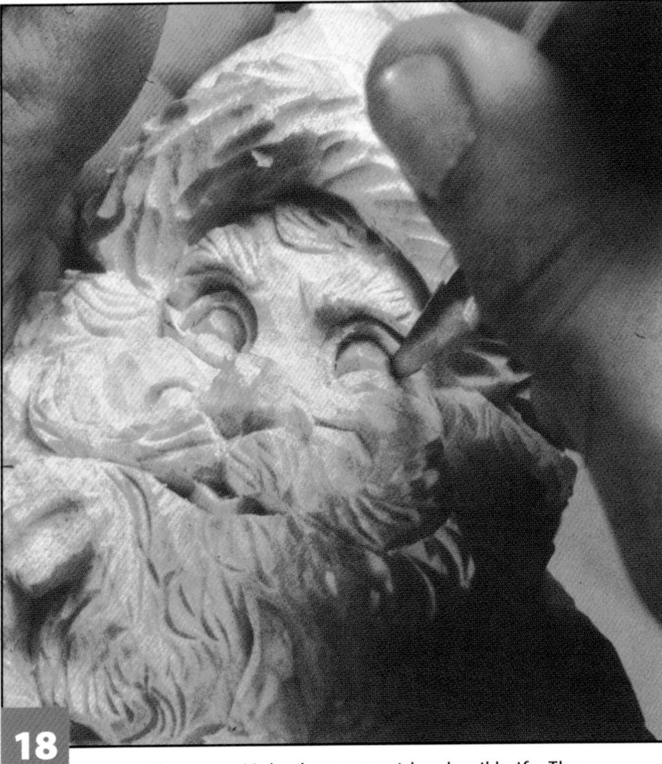

18 **Define the eyes.** Make deep cuts with a detail knife. The carving, not the painting, creates the expression in this carving.

19 **Clean up the eyes.** Some knife cuts leave behind fibers and fuzz. Use a woodburner on a medium setting to remove the fuzz.

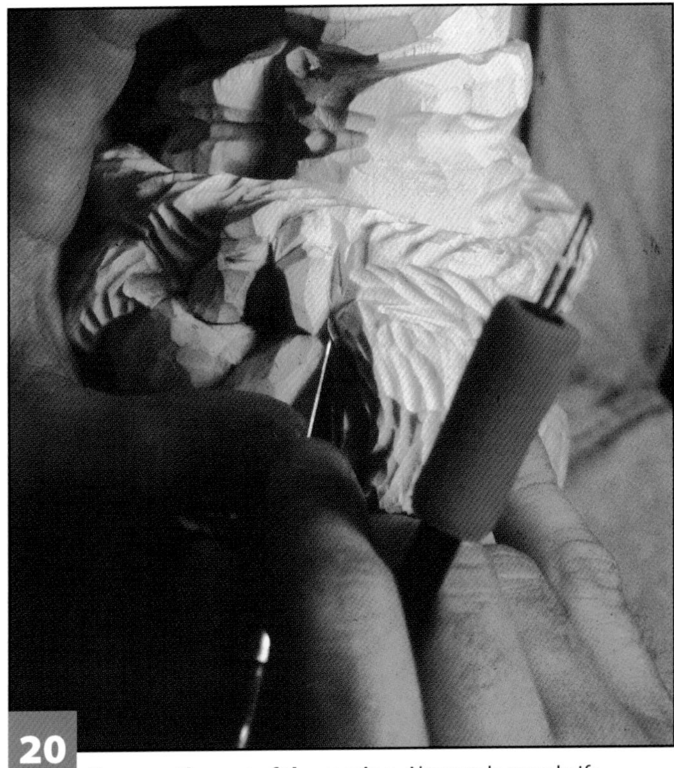

20 **Clean up the rest of the carving.** Alternately use a knife and woodburner to remove any fuzz or fibers from the other parts.

21 **Add depth to the wrinkles and undercuts.** Use a woodburner to deepen the cuts and add shadows.

painting notes

I use oil paints thinned with Minwax oil stain to add color and dimension to the carving.

THE FACE:

Mix a pink color for the face. Add highlights to the cheeks with red and use burnt sienna for the shadows. Use ultramarine blue for the irises of the eyes, black for the pupil, and white for the rest of the eye and to add a highlight dot to the pupil. Mix white, black and ultramarine blue to achieve a grey color for the beard.

THE COAT, HAT, AND PANTS:

Use red for all of these parts. Highlight the shadows with ultramarine blue.

THE BOOTS:

Paint the boots black. Highlight the shadows with ultramarine blue.

RUDOLPH:

Use brown ochre for the coat, and add white until it become a cream color for the spots. Paint the nose red.

Finish the carving with Deft semi-gloss spray lacquer.

materials & tools

MATERIALS:

5½" x 6" x 8" green white pine, basswood, or wood of choice

Minwax oil stain, natural

Oil paints: pink, red, burnt sienna, black, ultramarine blue, white, brown ochre

Deft semi-gloss spray lacquer

Paintbrushes of choice

TOOLS:

20mm #11 U-gouge

18mm #7 gouge

7mm # 9 gouge

4mm #11 gouge

3mm and 6mm V-tools

Carving knife of choice

Detail knife of choice

Spray bottle (if using green wood)

Woodburner with spear tip

About the Author

David Sabol is a world-renowned carver and member of the Caricature Carvers of America. Visit his website at www.davidsabol.com.

Right

Front

Left

Back

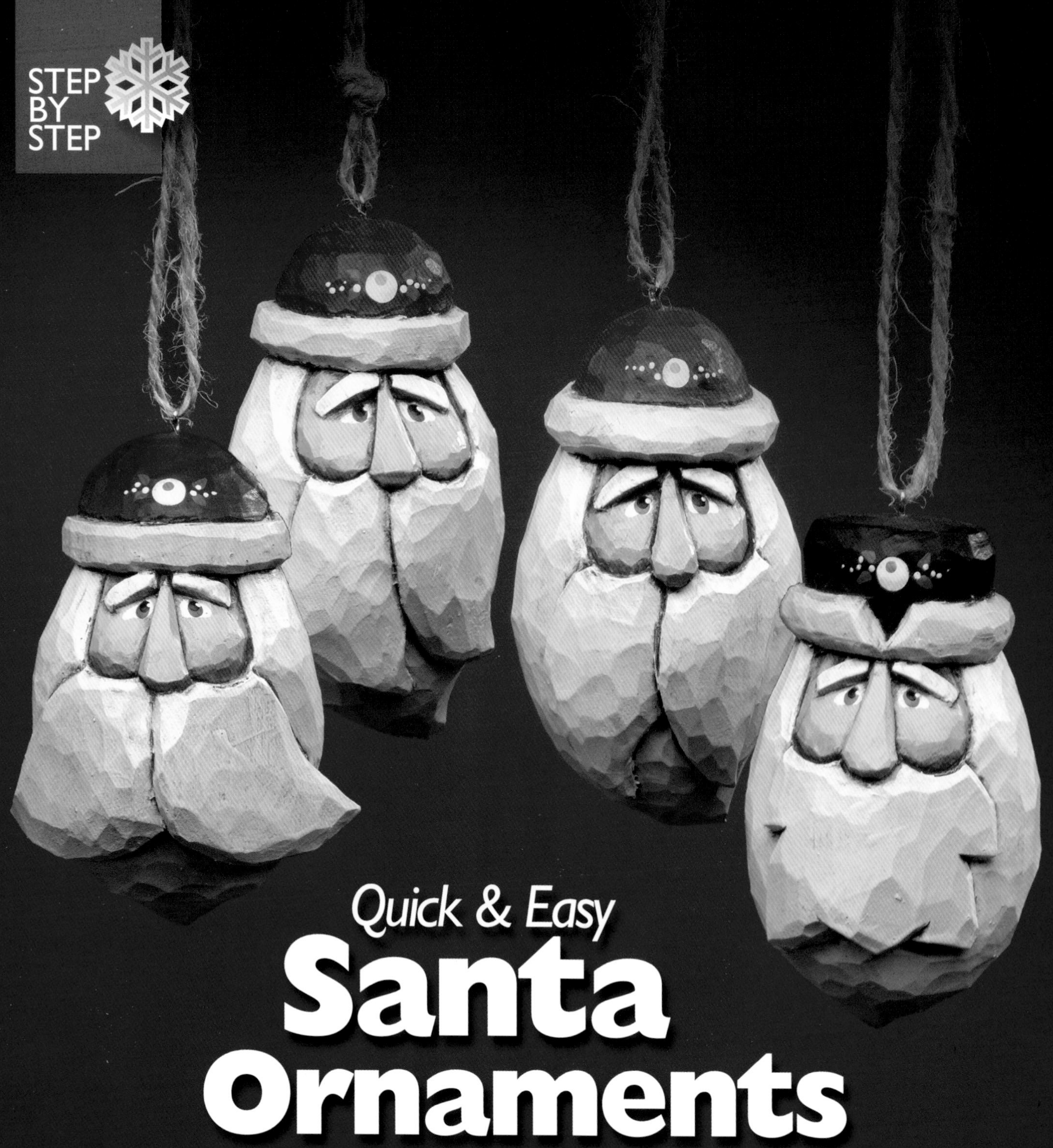

Quick & Easy Santa Ornaments

by Cyndi Joslyn

Because of their small size and simple cuts, these ornaments are perfect for beginner carvers. Experienced carvers can add subtle changes to the hat, hat trim, and beard to create an entire collection of Santa ornaments from one basic pattern. I recommend the use of a Kevlar carving glove and a carving apron to ensure your safety.

Start by transferring the pattern to the sides, top, and bottom of the blank, using transfer paper and a stylus.

1 **Score the top line on all sides of the wood with a bench knife.** With a gouge, slice off thin layers of wood, keeping the ledge you are creating flat. You do not want any hills or valleys. The resulting cylinder will become Santa's hat.

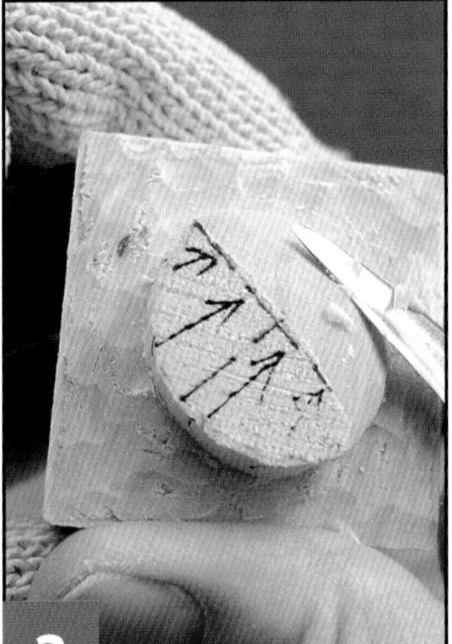

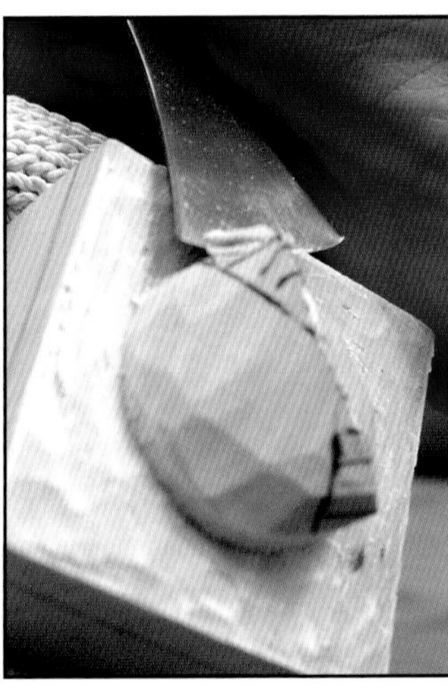

2 **Shape the hat.** Use a bench knife, gouge, or both to round the hat. You want to remove the squareness from the blank. Round the front and back of the hat up to the center line as shown above. Then carve off the square points on each side of the hat.

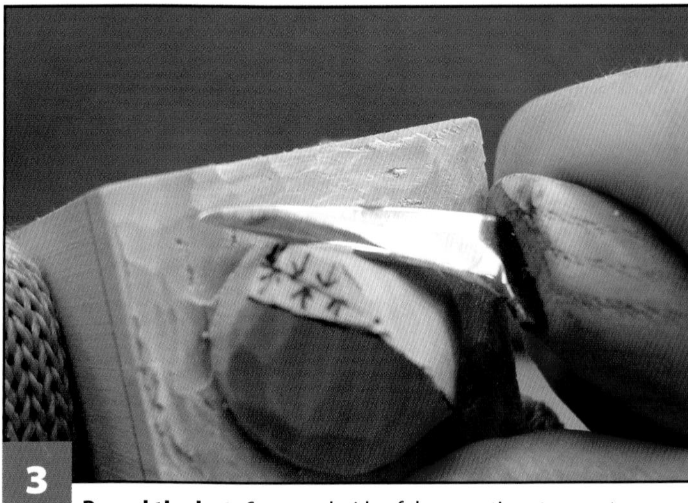

3 **Round the hat.** Carve each side of these sections to a center peak. Carve off the peak to round over the cap.

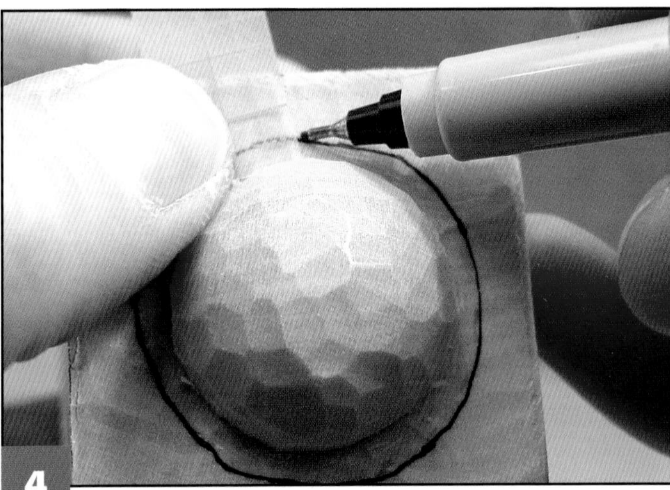

4 **Draw in the hat trim.** Measure out ⅛" from the base of the hat, and draw a circle around the hat.

5 **Carve in the hat trim.** Trim down to the next line indicated on the pattern using the circle drawn in Step 4 as a guide. Then score around the bottom edge of the hat trim.

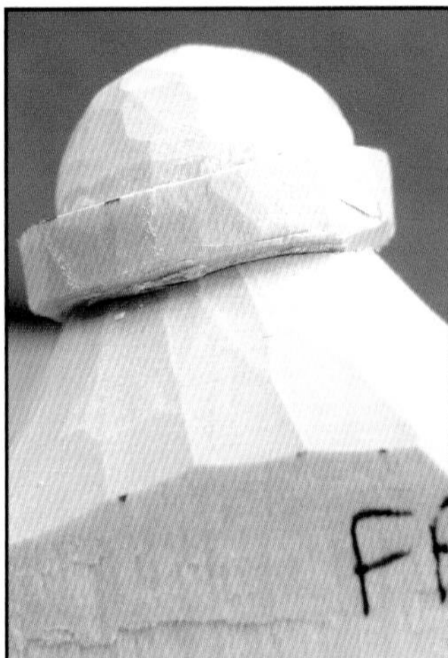

6 **Taper the head into the hat.** Make angled cuts to remove wood under the hat trim. This evenly rounded area extends approximately ¾" below the hat trim.

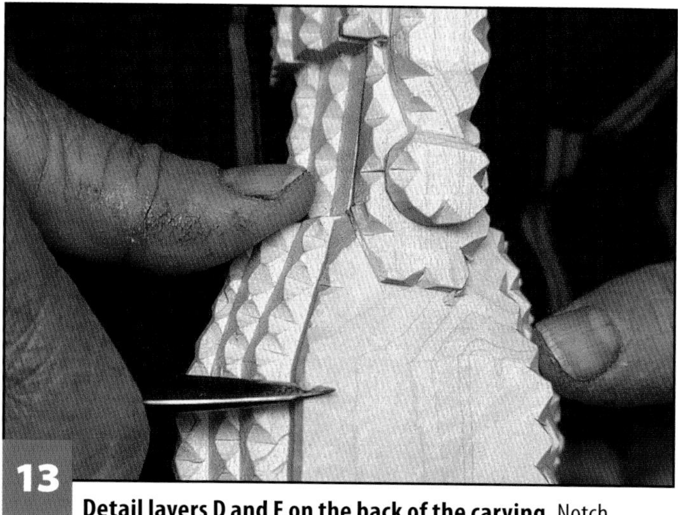

13 **Detail layers D and E on the back of the carving.** Notch the hat, hair, and perimeter of the coat on the back of the carving.

14 **Finish carving the facial features.** Small notches are cut on the beard and mustache.

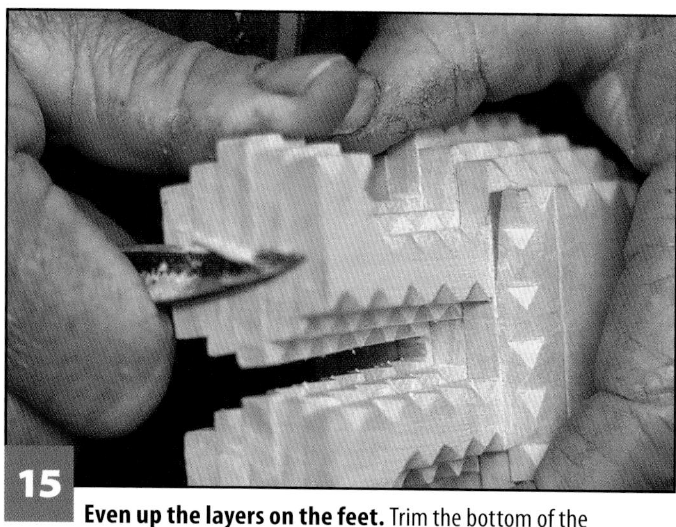

15 **Even up the layers on the feet.** Trim the bottom of the carving so the figure stands up straight. View the carving from all angles to make certain you didn't miss notching any areas.

16 **Outline the fur on Santa's coat.** Early tramp art carvers didn't have V-tools, but you can use one in place of a carving knife if you prefer. Apply thin traces of dry-brushed paint to the figure.

17 **Paint the eyes.** Use a small round-tip brush. Add a tiny dot of white paint on each pupil to suggest a reflection in the eyes.

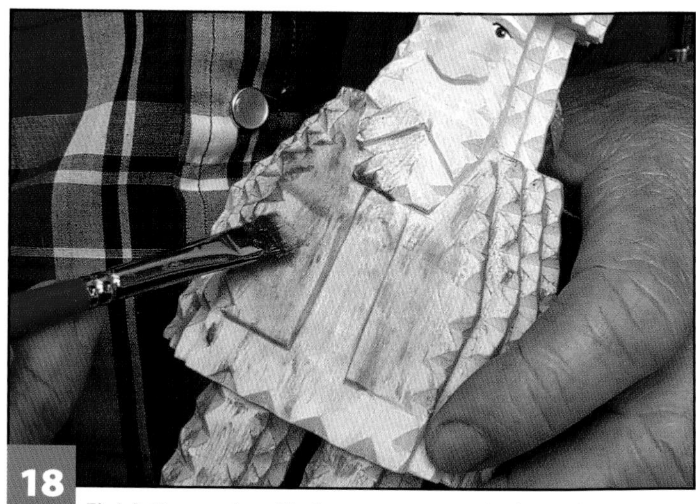

18 **Finish the carving.** The last step is to wax the finished figure, giving it the patina of a genuine antique tramp art piece.

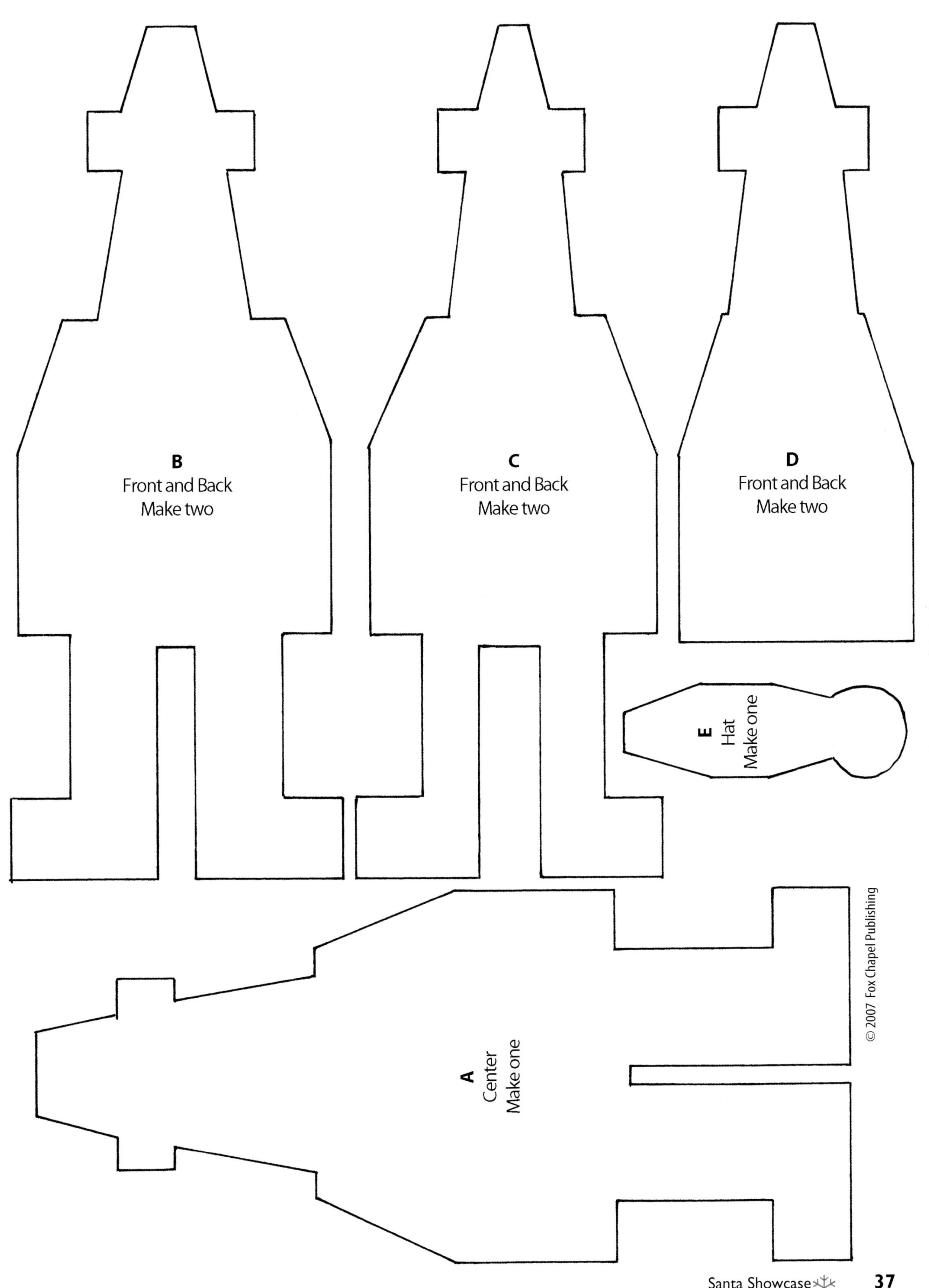
B
Front and Back
Make two
C
Front and Back
Make two
D
Front and Back
Make two
E
Hat
Make one
A
Center
Make one

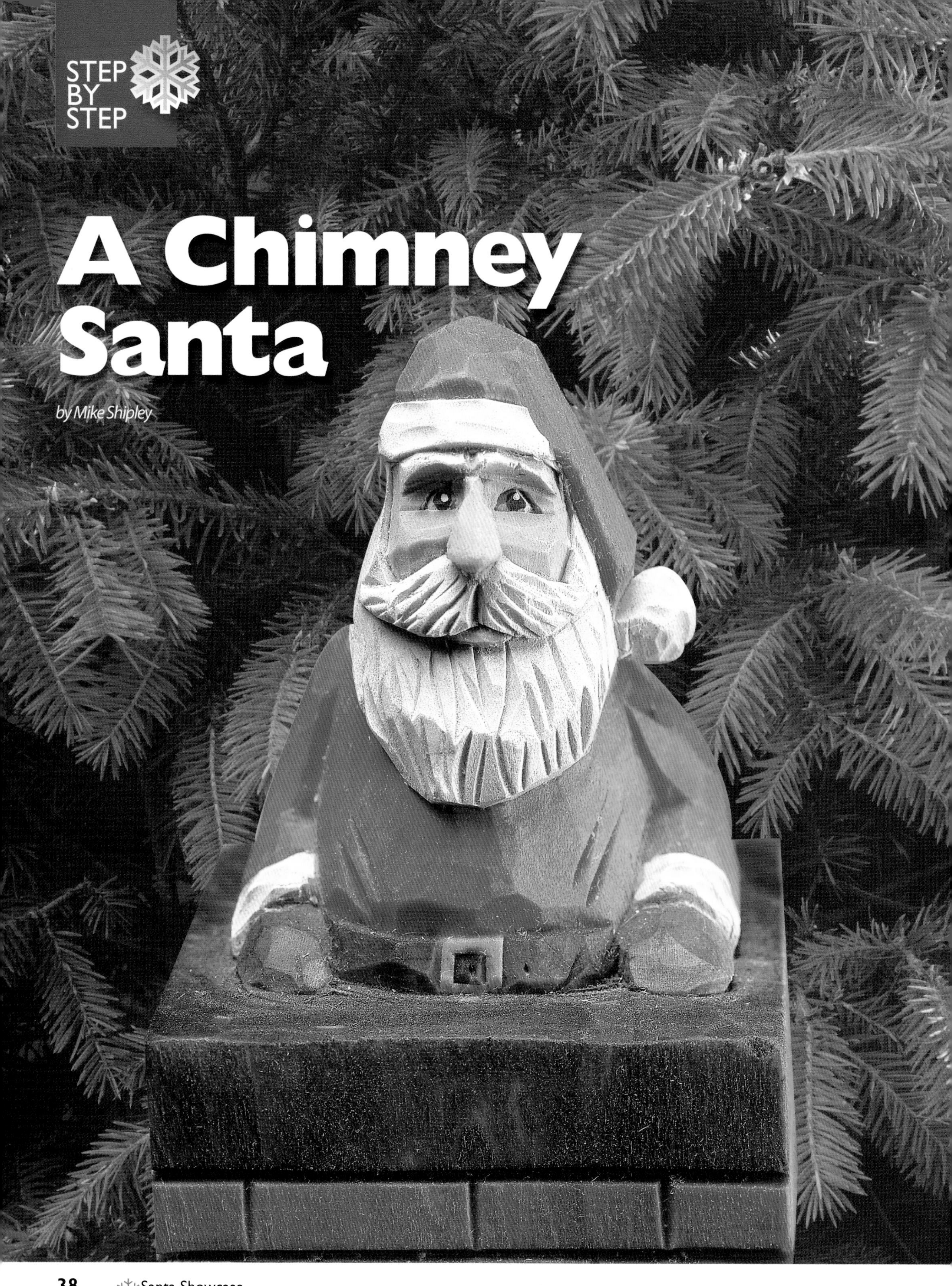

STEP BY STEP

A Chimney Santa

by Mike Shipley

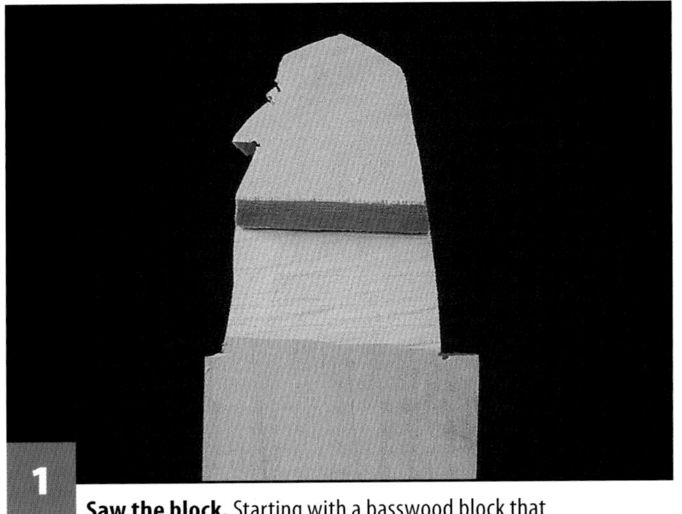

1 **Saw the block.** Starting with a basswood block that measures 2" square and 6" long, saw the side view first.

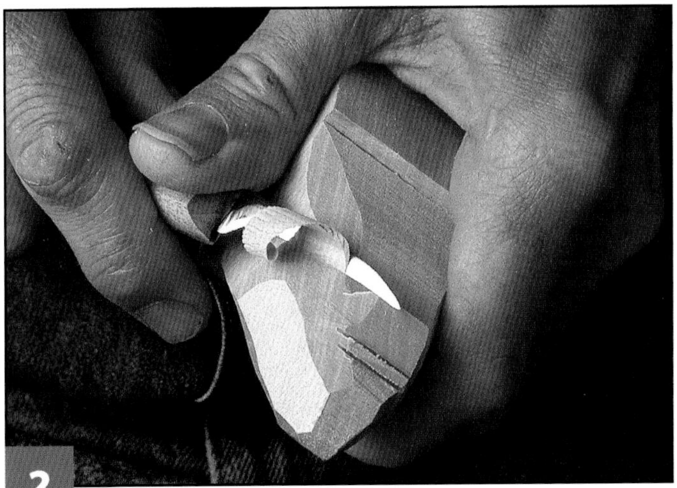

2 **Round out the Santa.** Leaving the chimney for later, start by rounding the body and head with a knife.

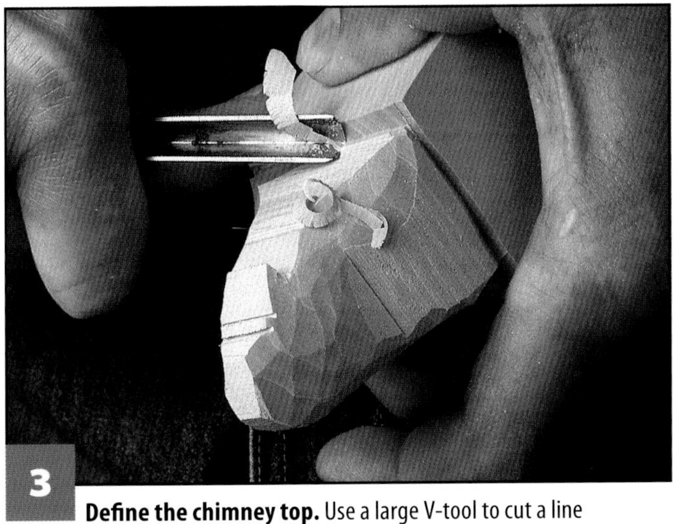

3 **Define the chimney top.** Use a large V-tool to cut a line around the top of the chimney. Make deeper cuts on the front and back; Santa's arms will rest on the sides of the chimney.

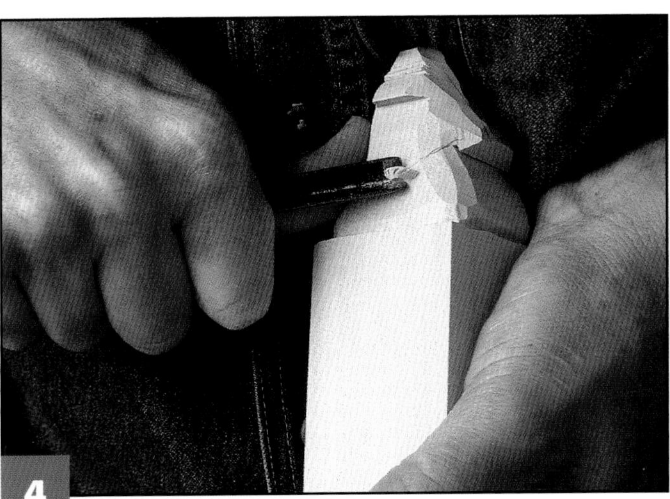

4 **Rough in the beard.** After penciling in the beard and hairline, cut the lines with a large V-tool. Make a deeper cut in the front to raise the beard.

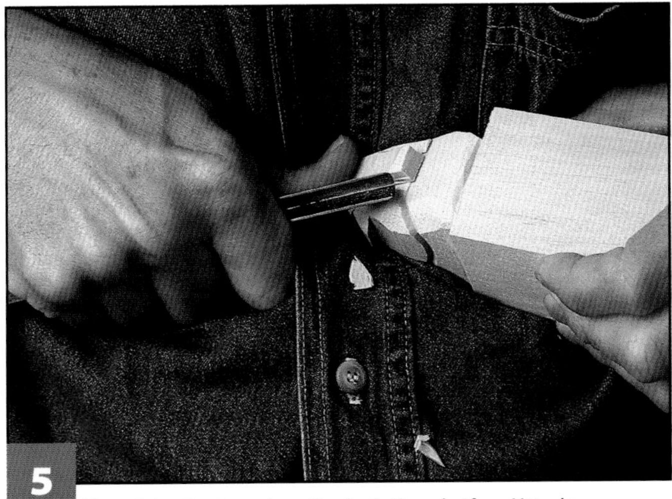

5 **Rough in the tassel on the hat.** Use a knife or V-tool to establish the basic shape.

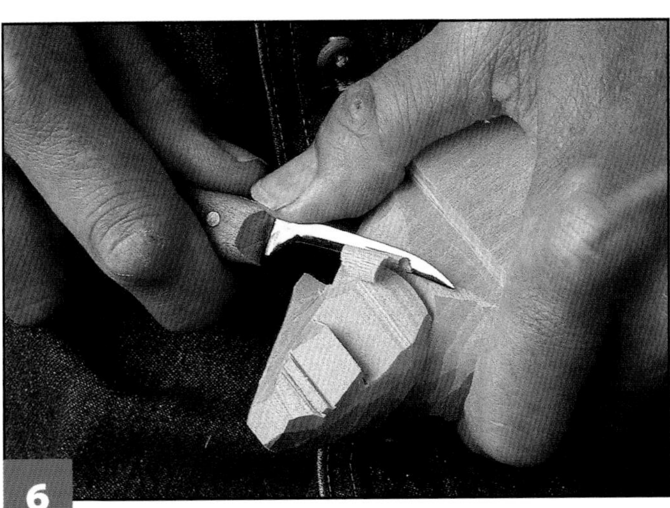

6 **Shape the body.** With a knife, clean up the body to the beard and to the hairline.

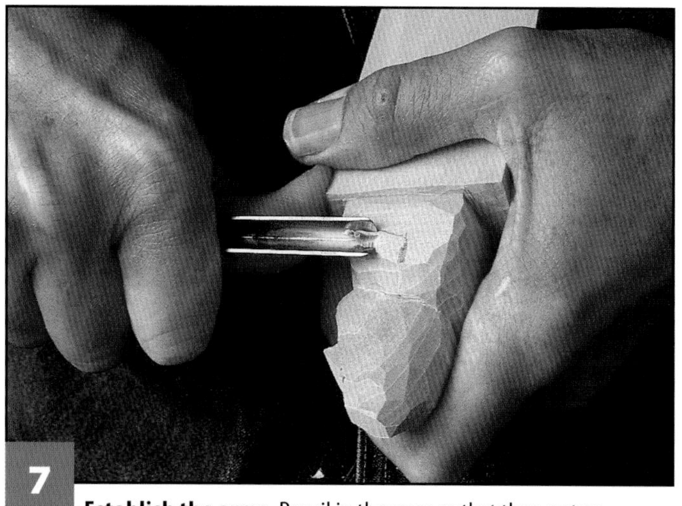

7 **Establish the arms.** Pencil in the arms so that they rest on top of the chimney. Rough in the arms with a large V-tool.

8 **Shape the arms.** With a knife, clean up the arms to their finished size.

9 **Sketch in the details on the back of the carving.** Pencil in the arm lines on the back and the hat line around the head. Use a small V-tool to set in the lines.

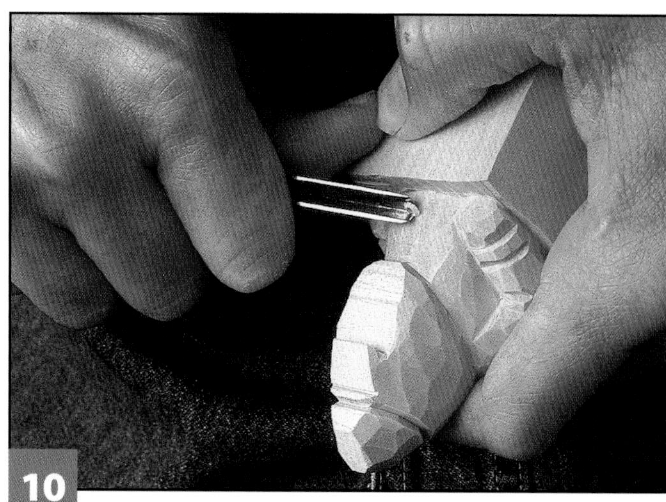

10 **Define the clothing.** With a small V-tool, cut the hat line, the cuffs on the coat sleeves, and the belt in front and back. The mittens are simply rounded with no thumbs showing.

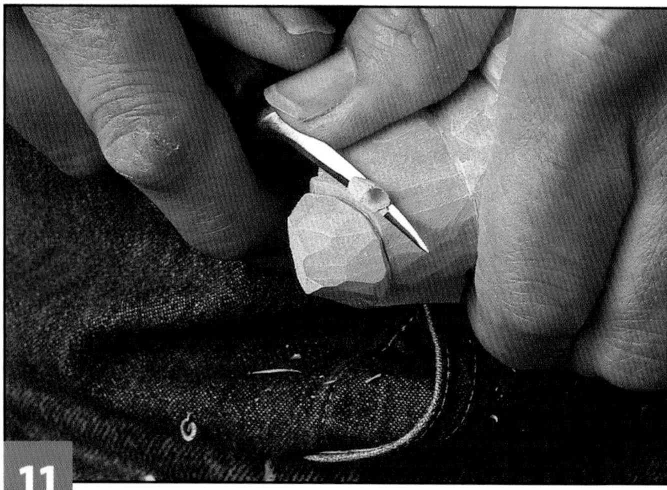

11 **Shape the back of the head.** With a knife, carve the back of the head to its finished size.

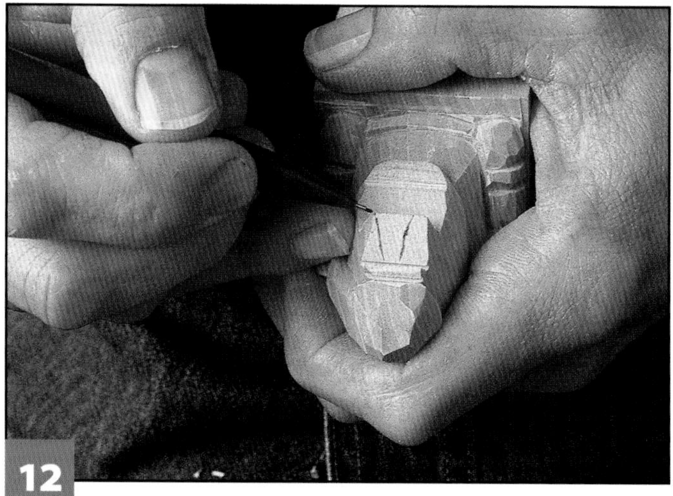

12 **Define the nose.** Pencil in the nose. It has a triangular shape with the widest part on the bottom.

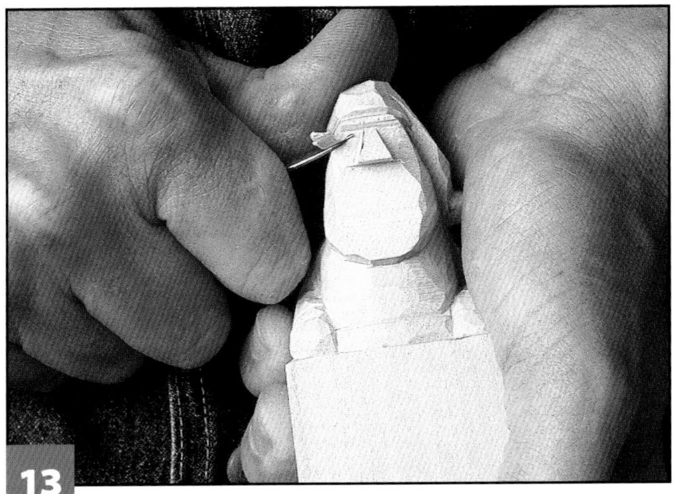

13 **Shape the nose.** Using a knife, remove wood on both sides of the nose. Clean up the face area and cut away the bottom corners of the nose.

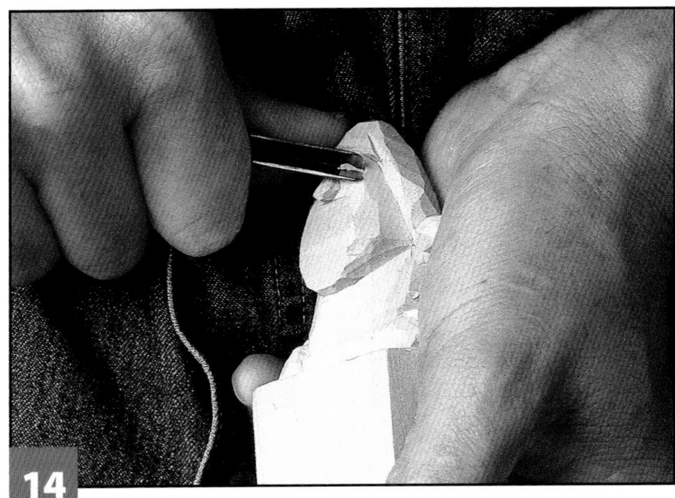

14 **Add the eyebrows.** With a small V-tool, cut in under the eyebrows on both sides of the nose. Work to keep both sides of the face symmetrical.

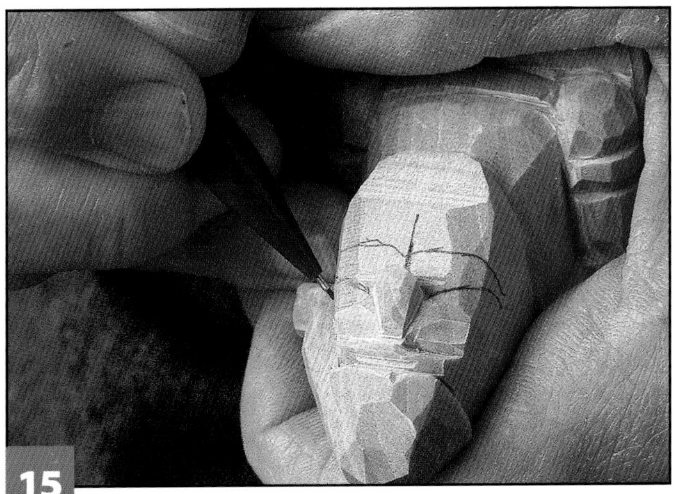

15 **Define the mustache.** Pencil in the mustache using the pattern as a guide.

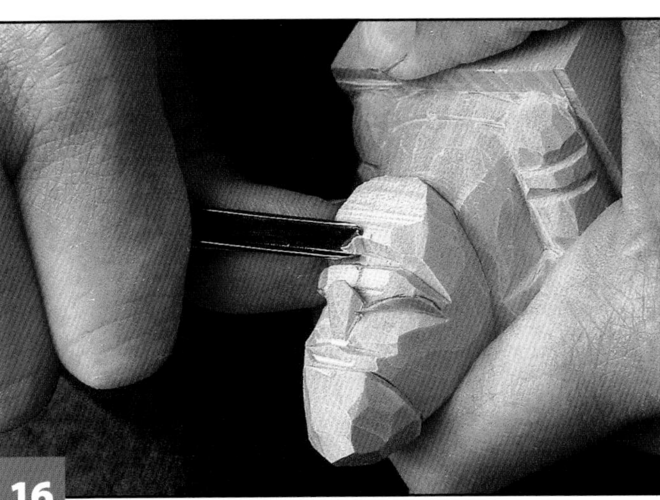

16 **Shape the mustache.** With a small V-tool, outline the mustache, cutting deeply enough to raise it above the face.

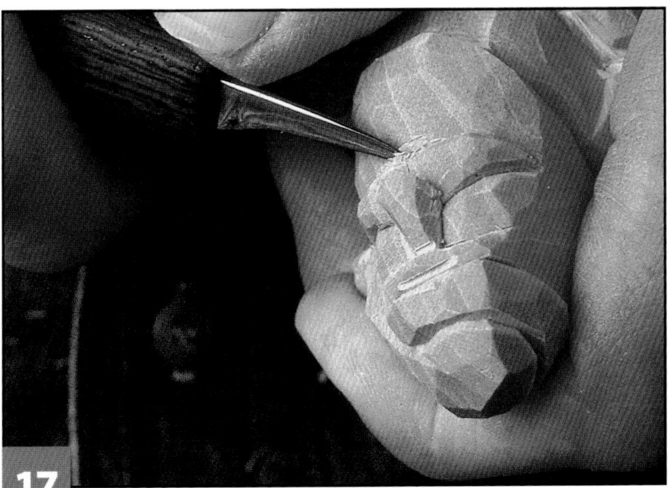

17 **Clean up the features.** Use a knife to clean up the beard, face, and mustache. Then carve a simple, rounded mouth.

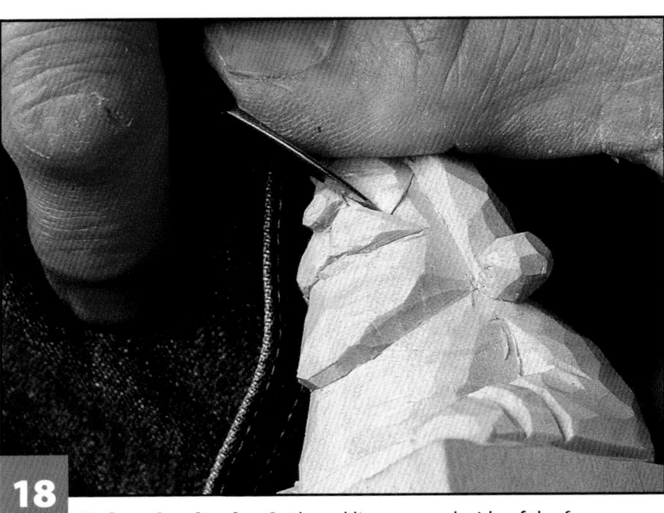

18 **Define the cheeks.** Cut beard lines on each side of the face with a knife. Cut away the cheeks to raise the beard off the face.

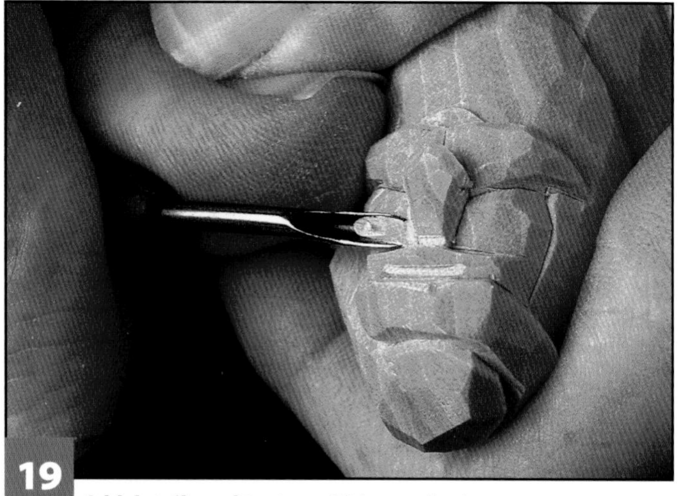

19 **Add details and texture.** With a small veiner, scoop out the eye sockets and the nostrils under the nose. Use the same tool to make shallow cuts for fur on the tassel, hat fringe, and cuffs.

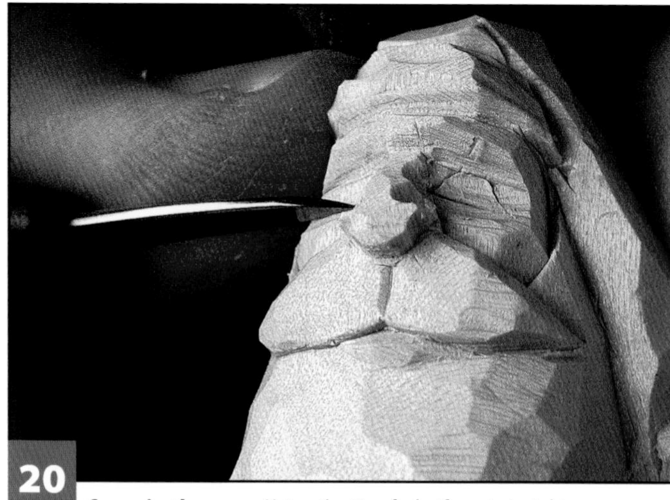

20 **Carve in the eyes.** Using the tip of a knife, cut straight, horizontal lines on both sides of the nose. Cut half moons above the lines. Trim the inside corners to slightly round the eyeballs.

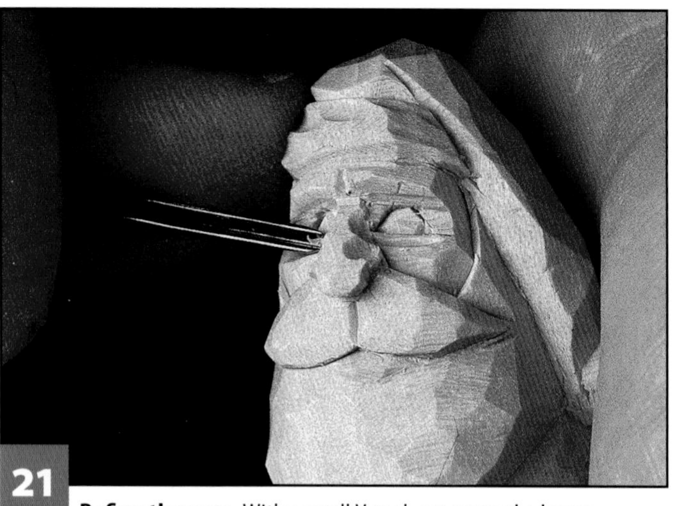

21 **Refine the eyes.** With a small V-tool, cut across the lower eyelids, just below the horizontal line, to give the eyelids a slightly raised appearance.

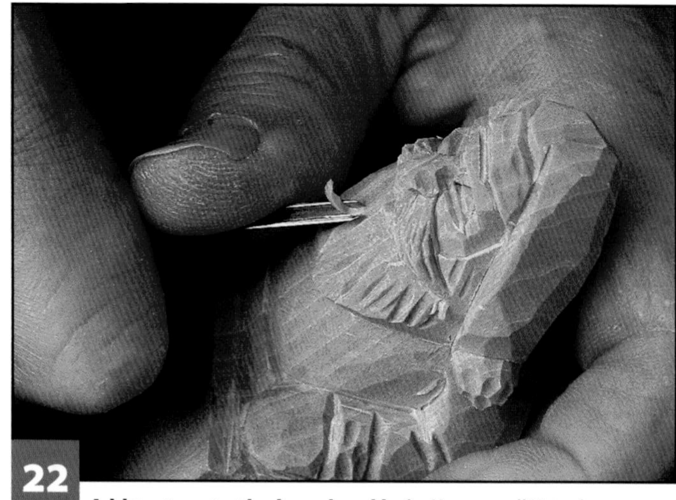

22 **Add texture to the beard and hair.** Use a small V-tool to cut the whiskers and hair, making long and short cuts that are either straight or curved to give the appearance of hair.

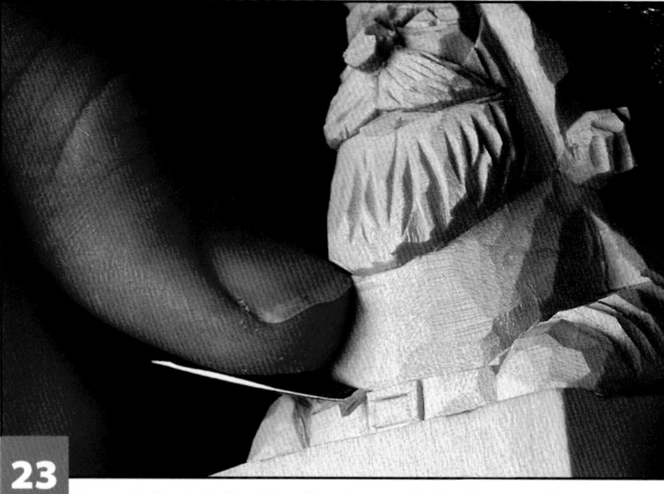

23 **Detail the belt buckle.** Use the tip of a knife to establish a belt buckle, centered between Santa's hands. I make two rectangles, one inside the other.

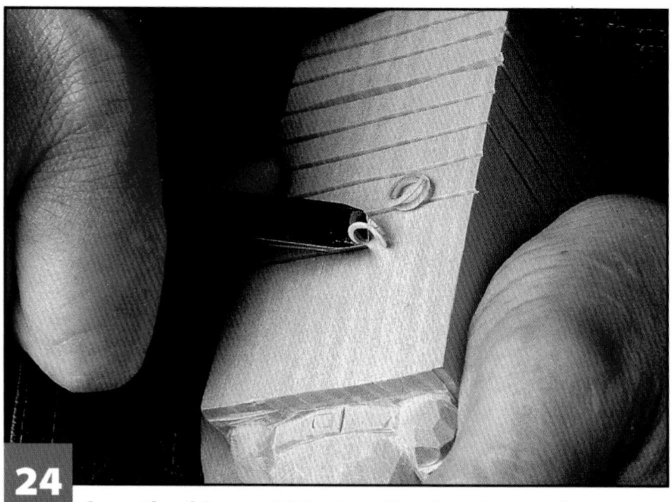

24 **Carve the chimney.** With a large V-tool, cut horizontal brick lines on all sides of the chimney. These lines don't have to be perfect. Slightly crooked lines give the bricks a weathered look.

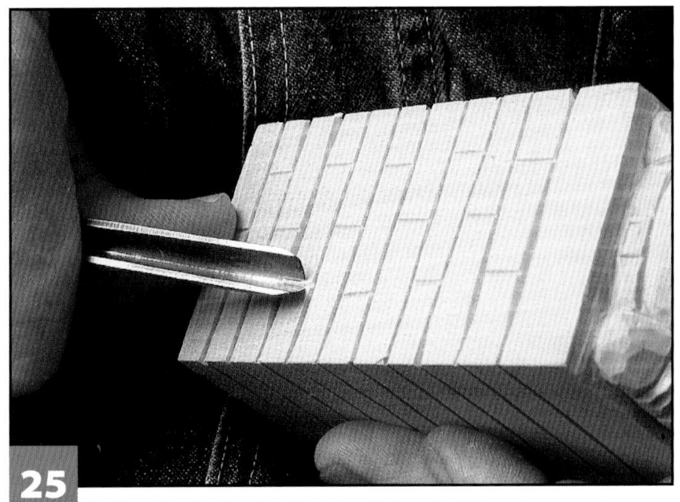

25 **Define the individual bricks.** Cut vertical lines to separate the bricks with a V-tool. Stagger the lines from row to row.

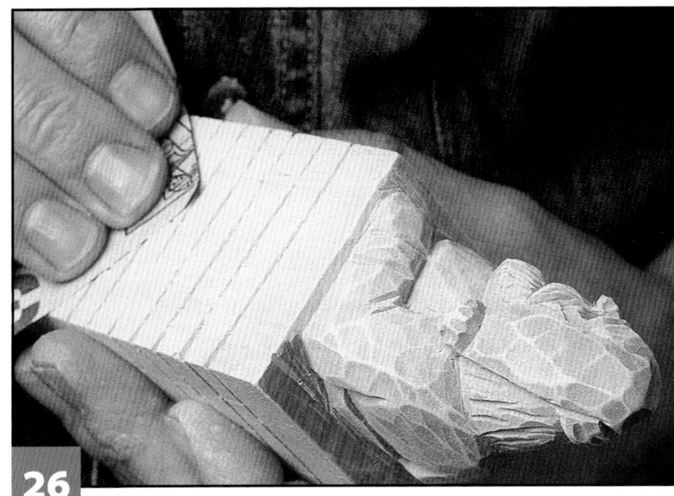

26 **Lightly sand the chimney.** Use 220-grit sandpaper. This helps to give the bricks the appearance of age.

27 **The carving is finished.** Look over the entire carving for any areas that need attention before painting.

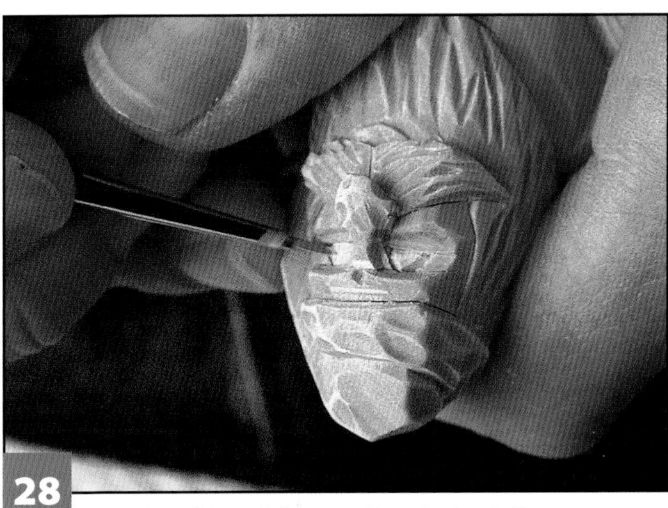

28 **Paint the whites of the eyes.** Use a fine brush. To ensure good coverage, do not thin the white paint too much.

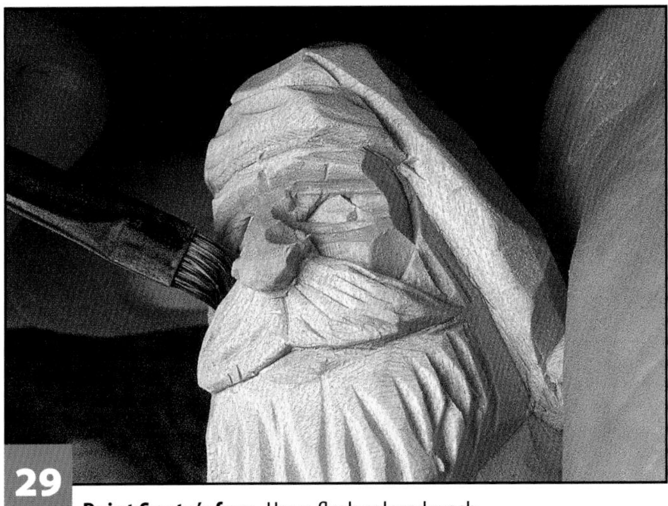

29 **Paint Santa's face.** Use a flesh colored wash.

30 **Paint the mittens.** Use a pale green wash.

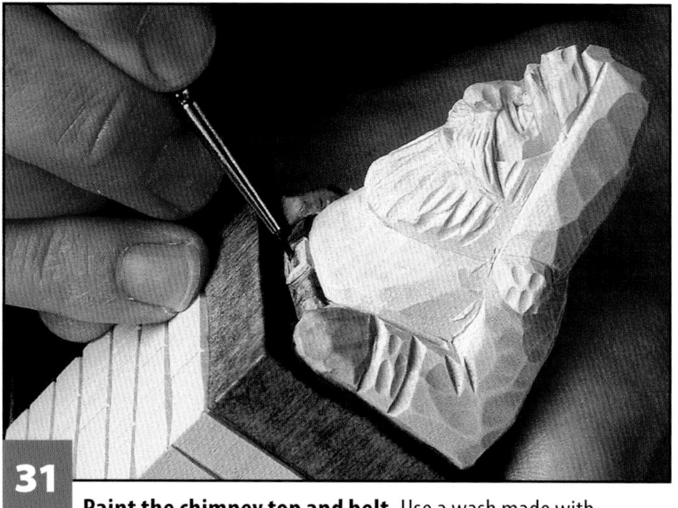

31 Paint the chimney top and belt. Use a wash made with black paint. Avoid the belt buckle.

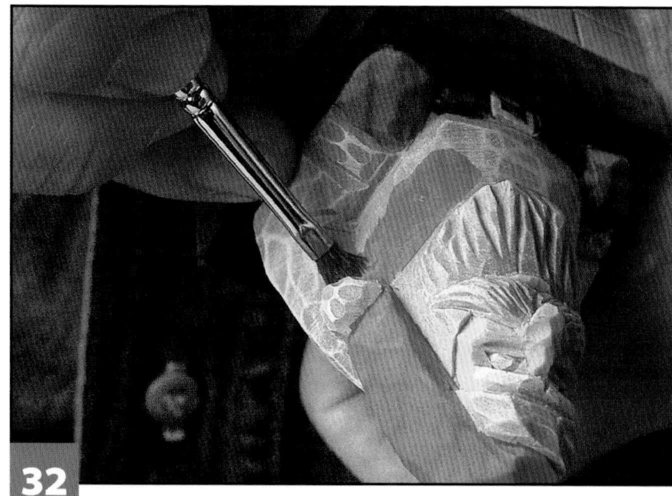

32 Paint the clothing and hair. Use cadmium red medium for the hat and coat. Use white for the beard, hair, and clothing trim.

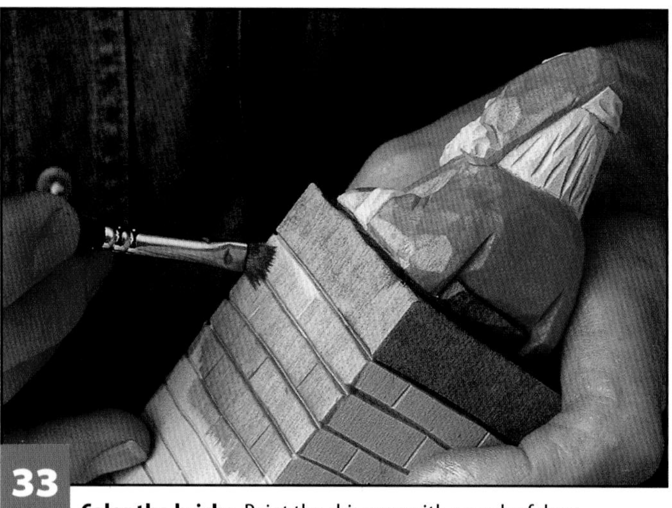

33 Color the bricks. Paint the chimney with a wash of deep red. Be sure to get deep into the brick lines to help separate the bricks and add definition.

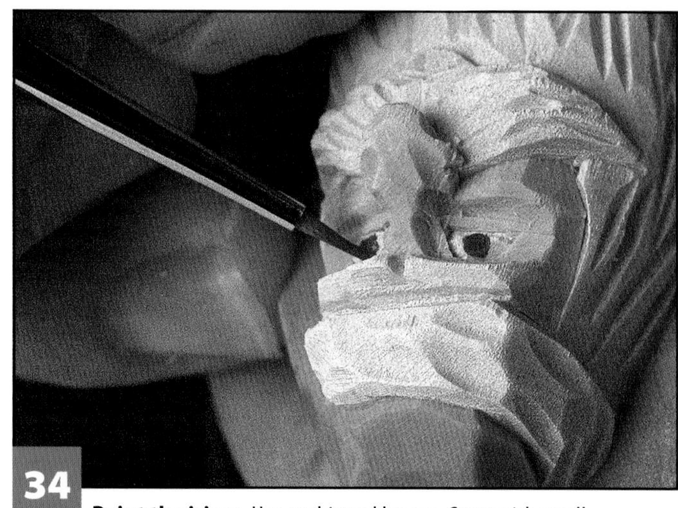

34 Paint the irises. Use unthinned brown. Start with small dots in the centers of the eyeballs and enlarge them until the eyes have a natural and relaxed look.

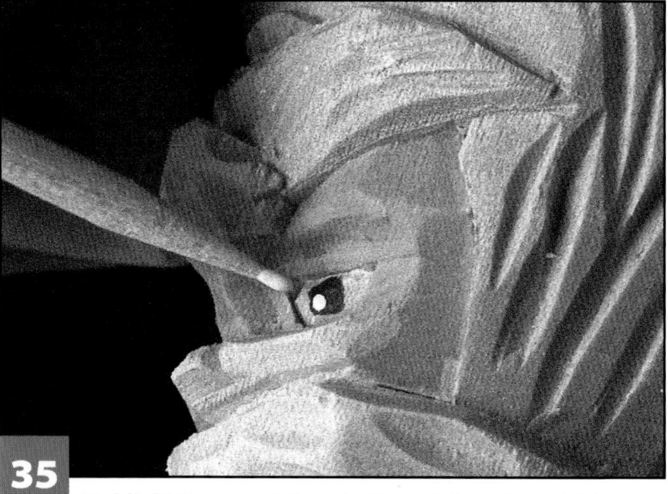

35 Highlight the eyes. Using a toothpick, take white straight from the tube or container and place a small dot of color on each eyeball to add a twinkle to Santa's eyes.

36 Stain the carving. Allow the paint to dry for 30 minutes before staining. Dip the entire carving into a mix of boiled linseed oil and raw umber oil paint. Dry off the carving with paper towels.

Right

Front

Left

Back

Basket Santa

ART SHOEMAKER

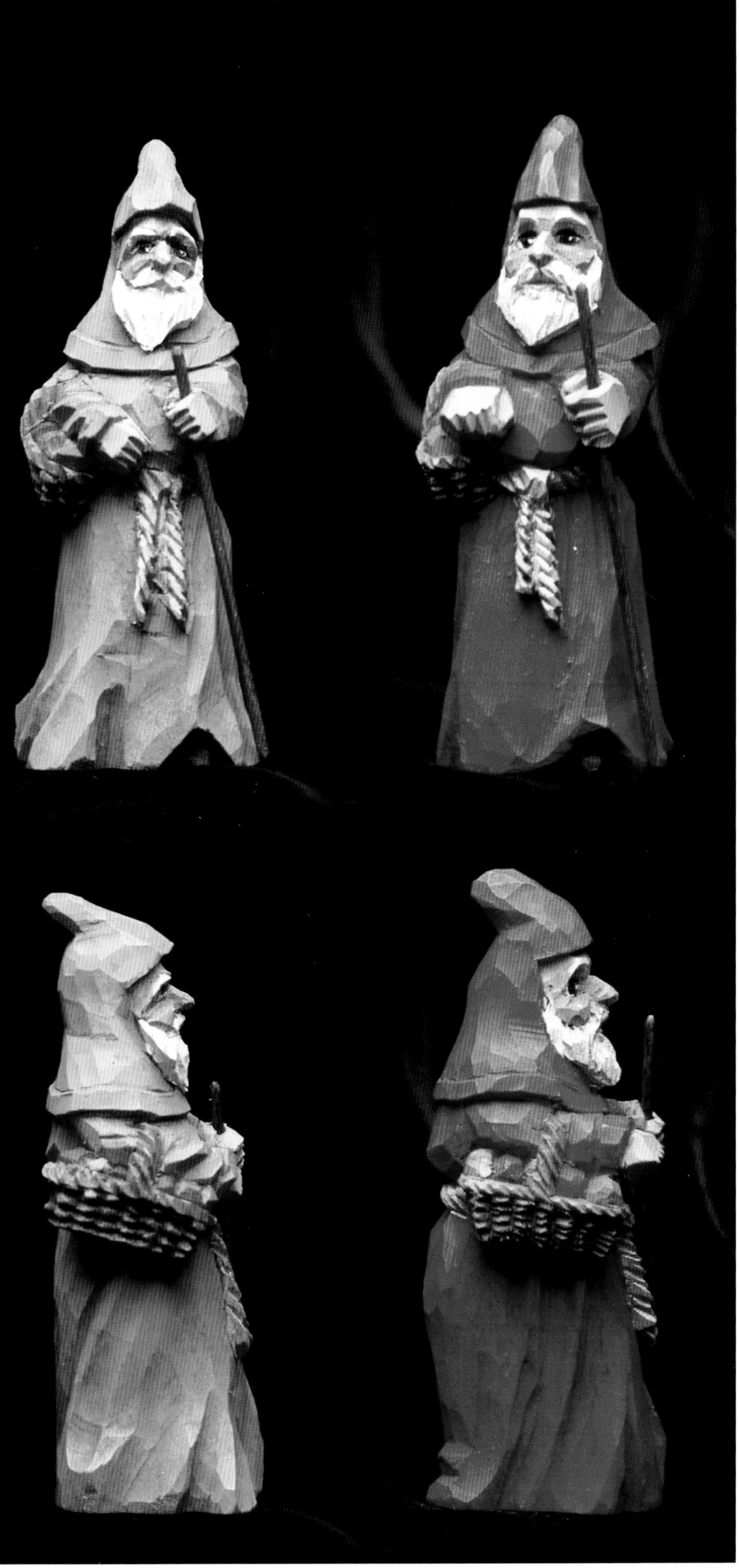

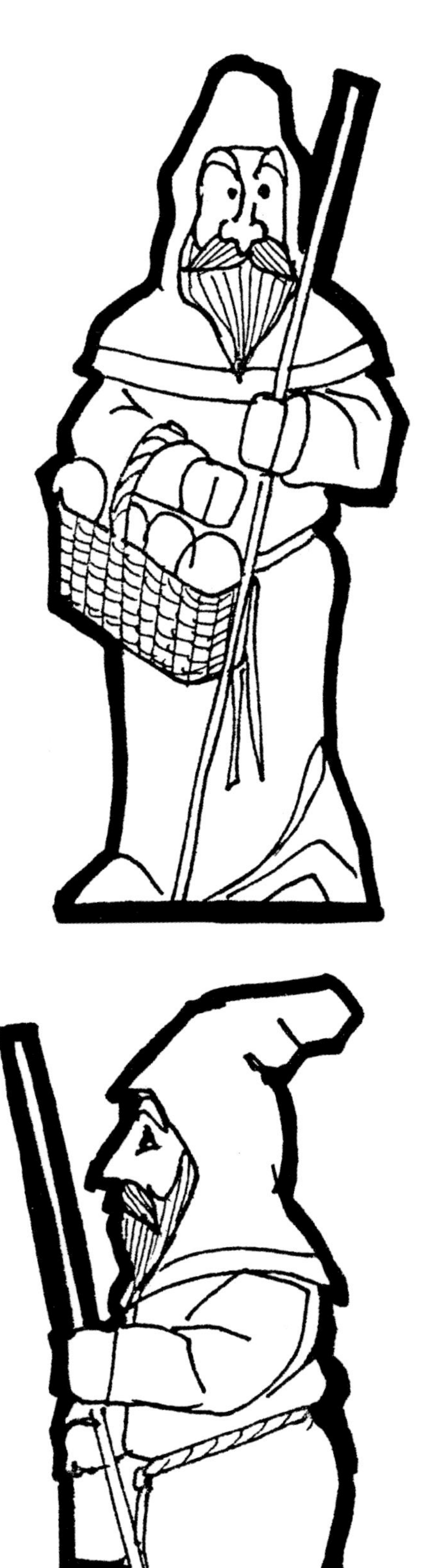

European Santa

ART SHOEMAKER

Apple Santa

TINA TONEY

Olde World Santa

JOEL HULL

Right

Left

Back

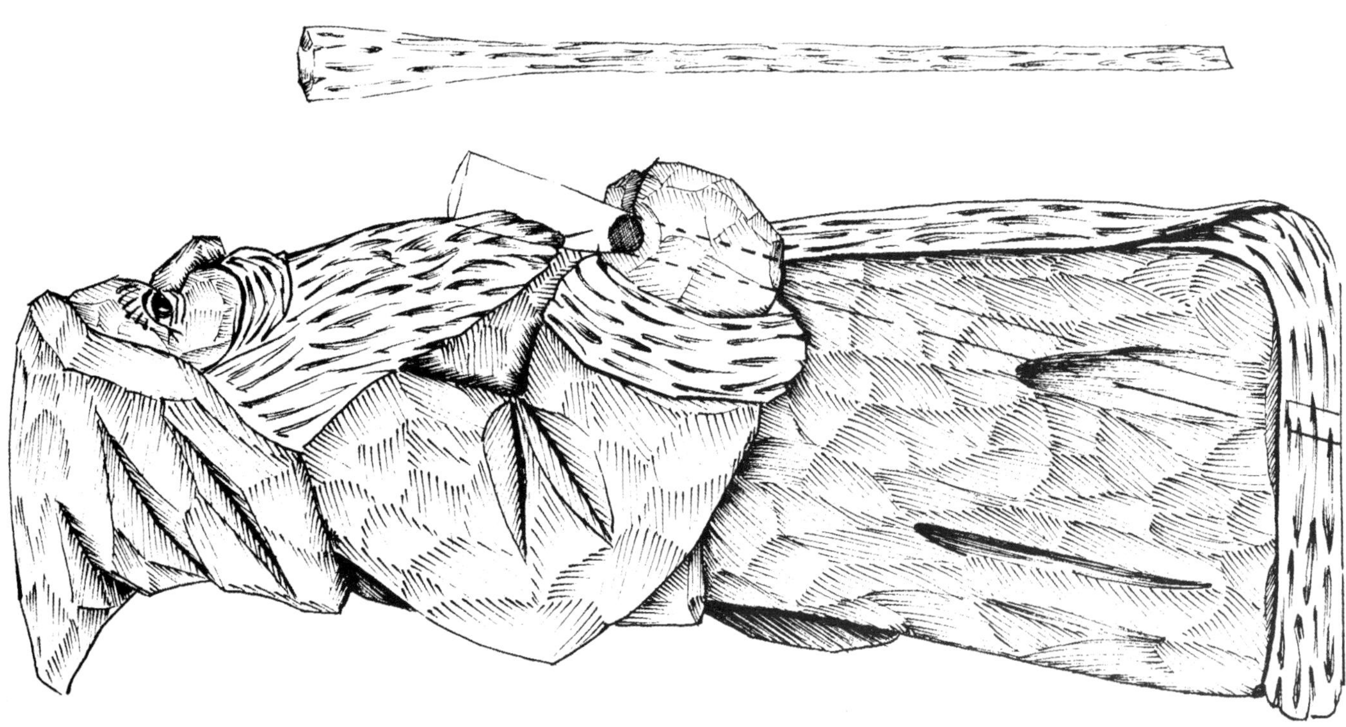

Stackable Santa

JOHN RICHARDSON

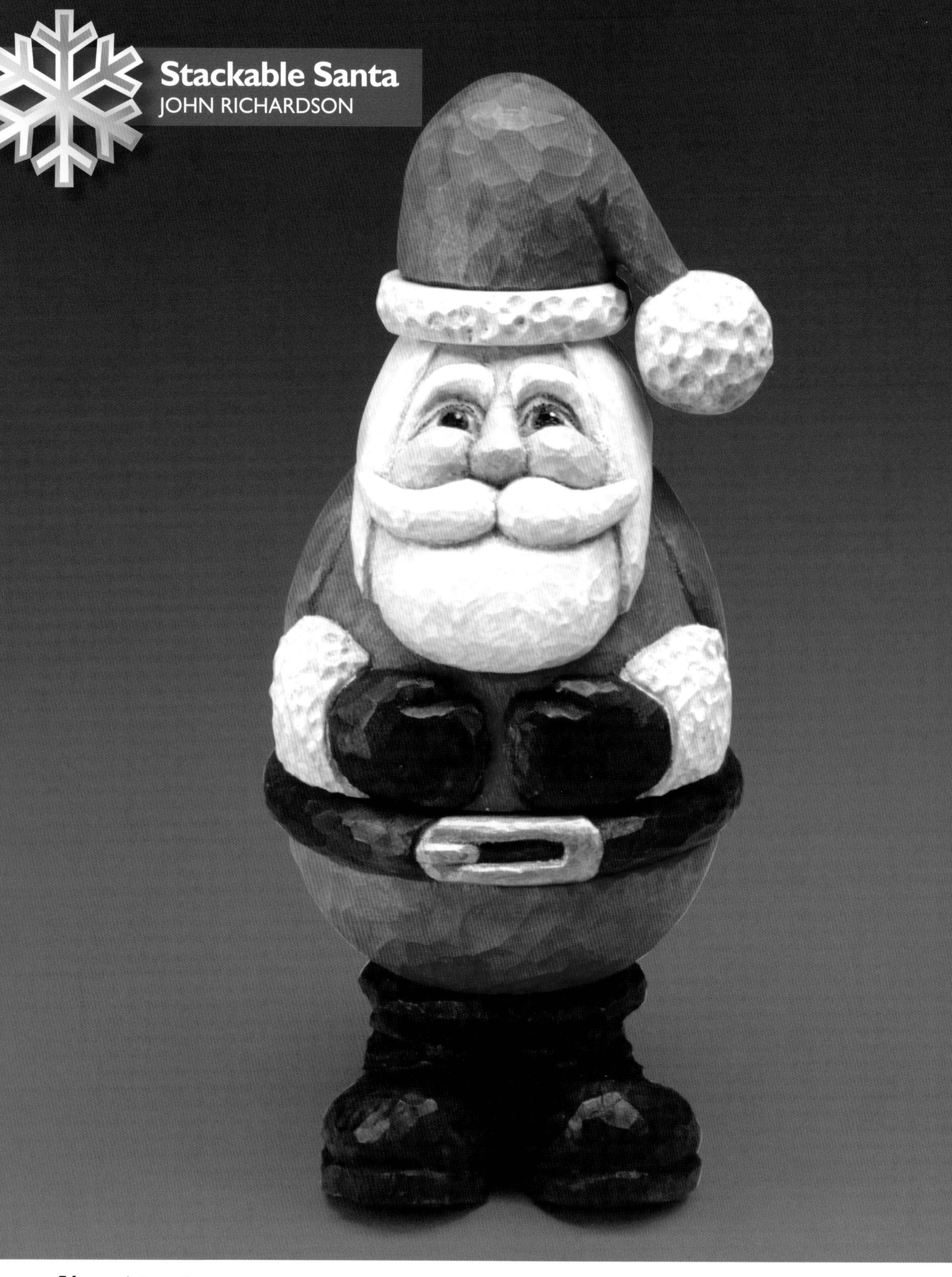

Carving different segments lets you customize the look of your Santa.

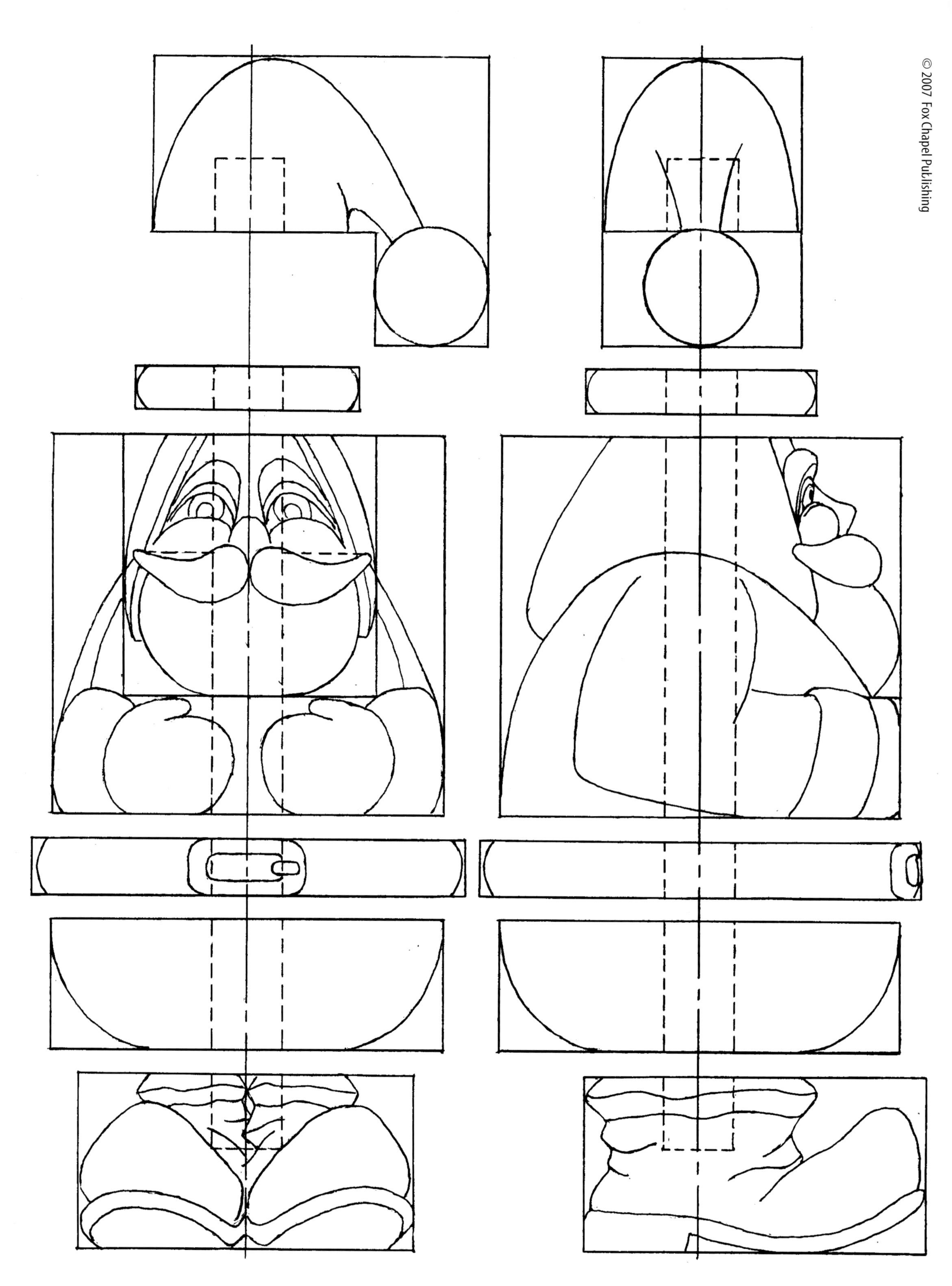

Santa's Gift
MARK KLEIN

Biker Santa

SUE MADSEN

Woodland Santa

JANET CLEMENS

Santa Egghead

JIM FARR

 Illustrator: Jack Kochan

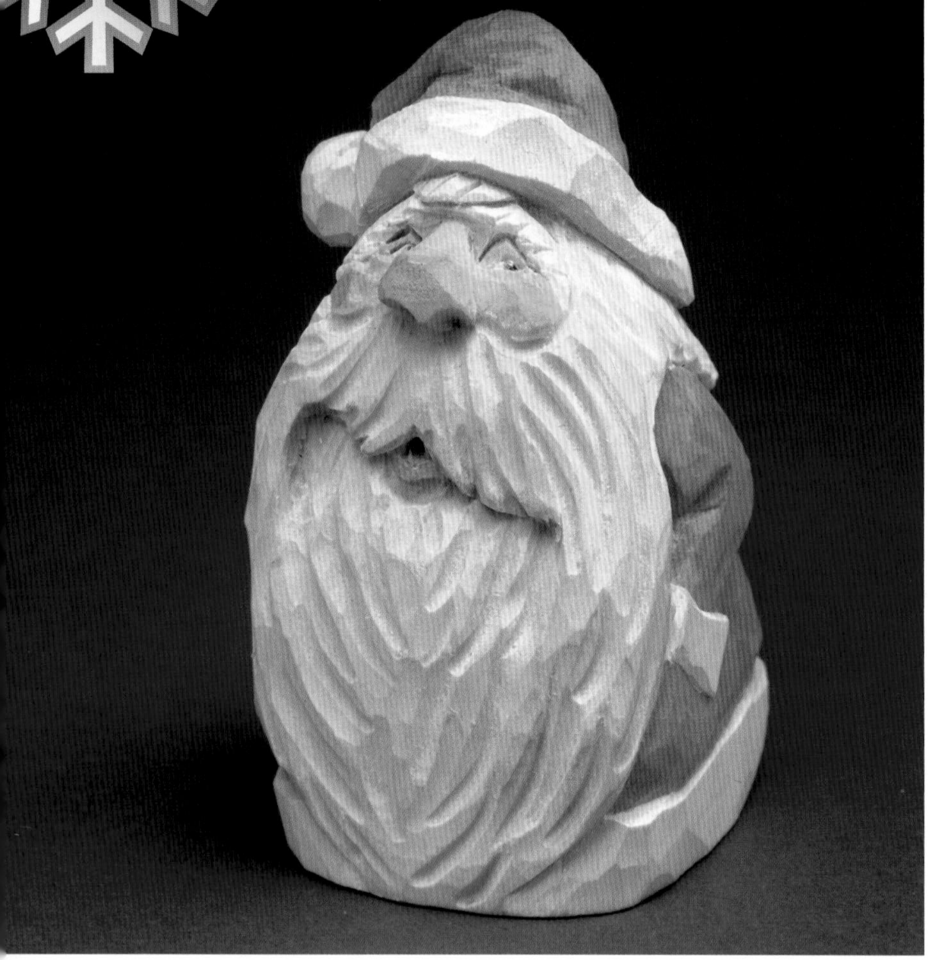

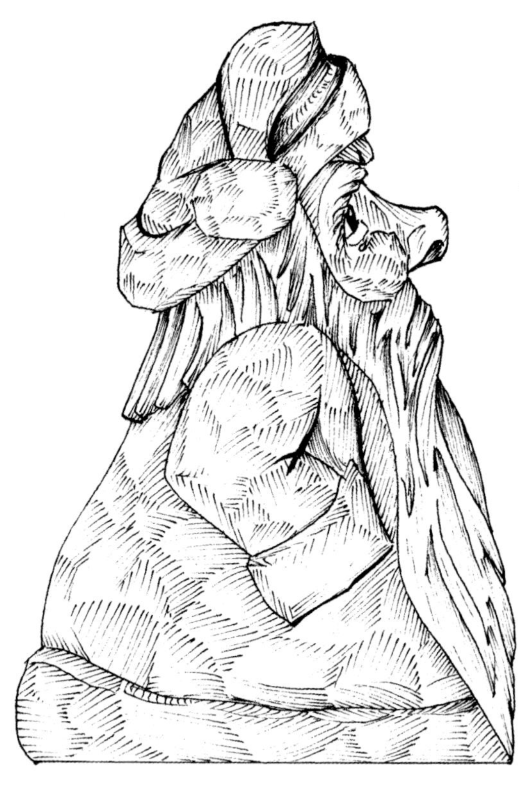

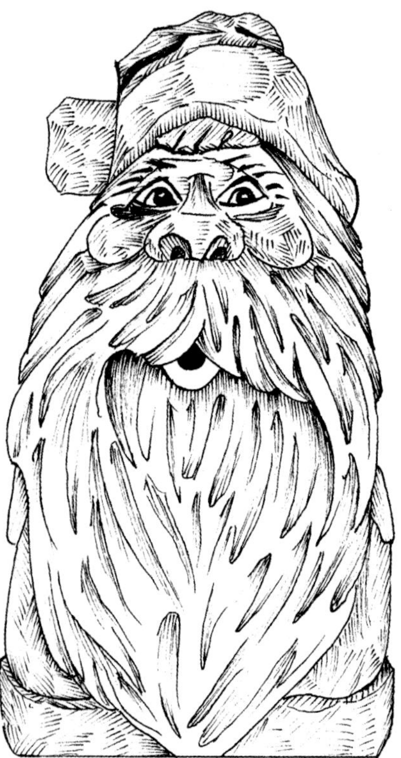

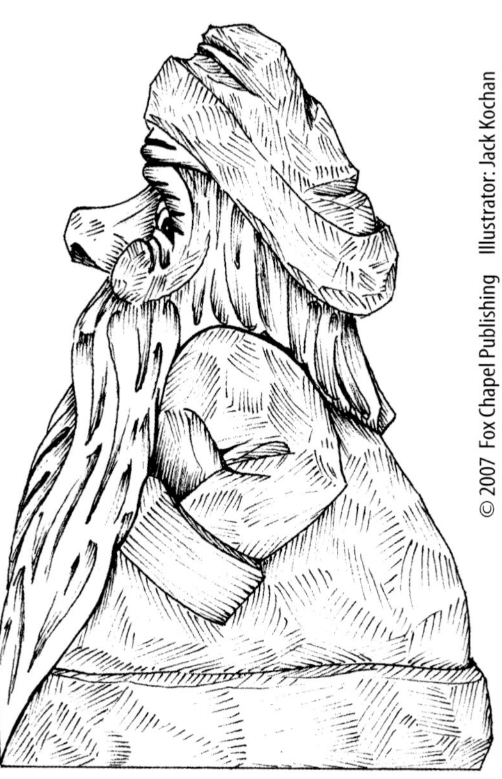

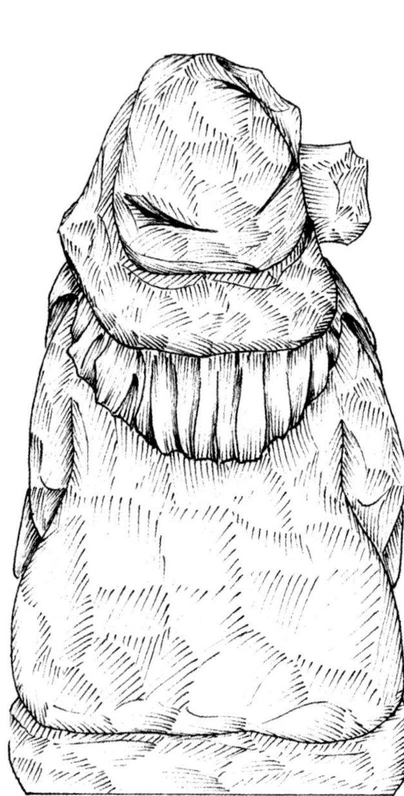

Father Christmas

NORB HARTMANN

Right

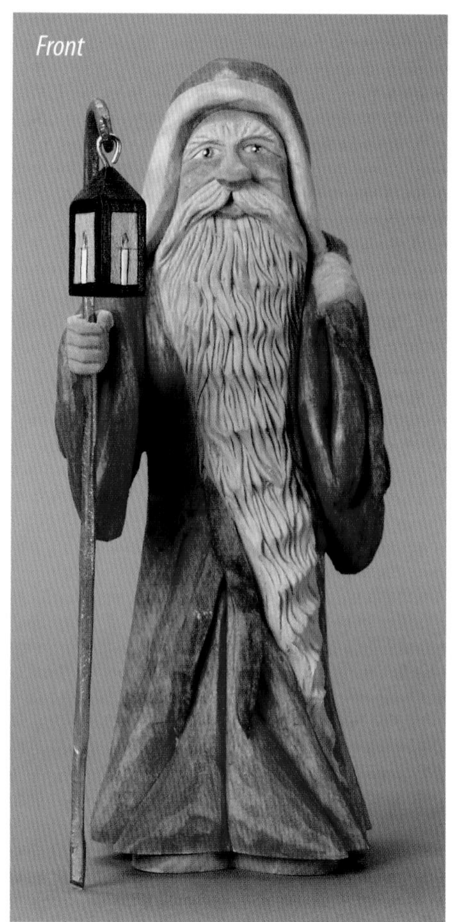
Front

Left

Back

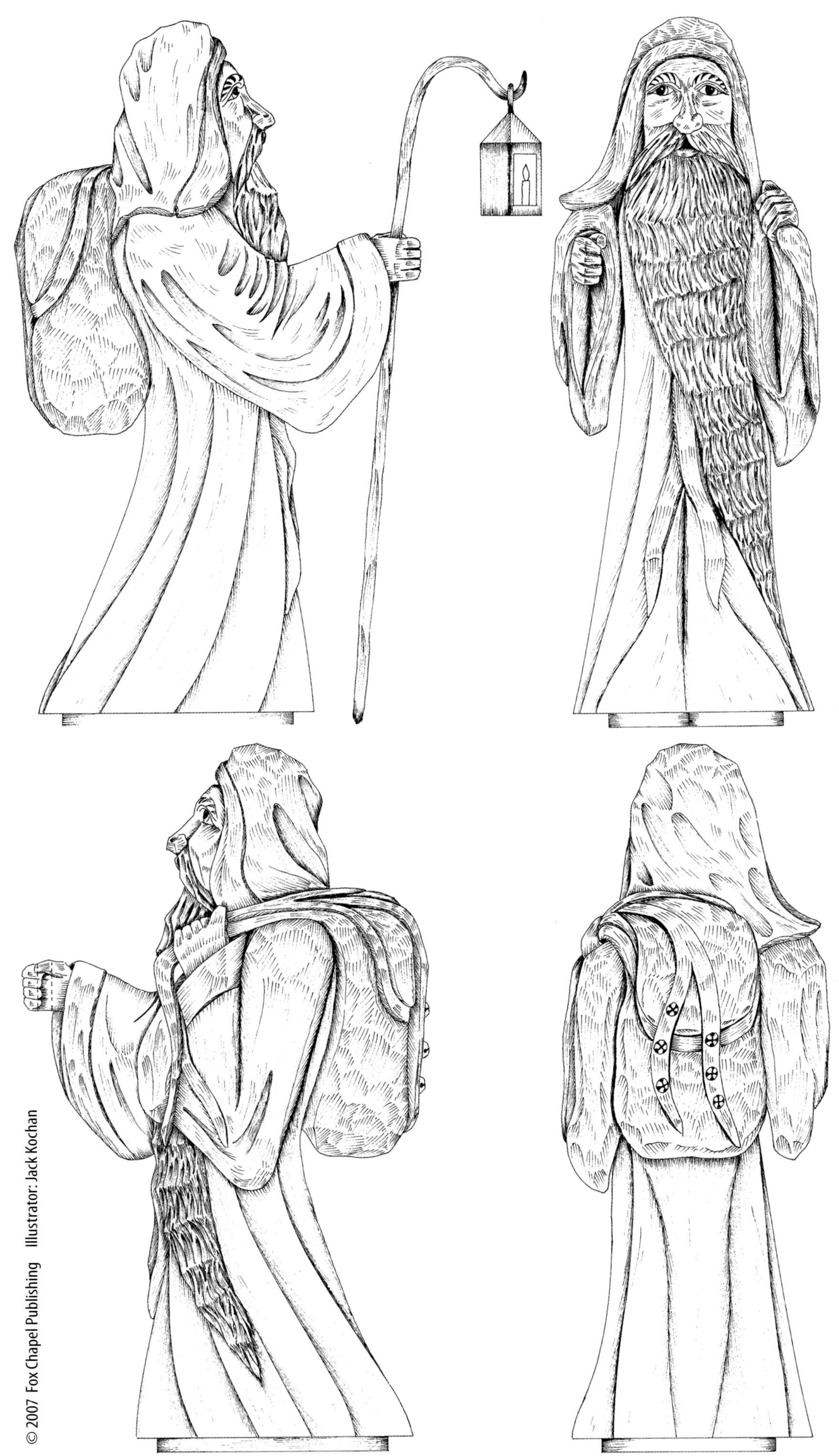

Lost in Thought

WAYNE SHINLEVER

Right

Front

Left

Back

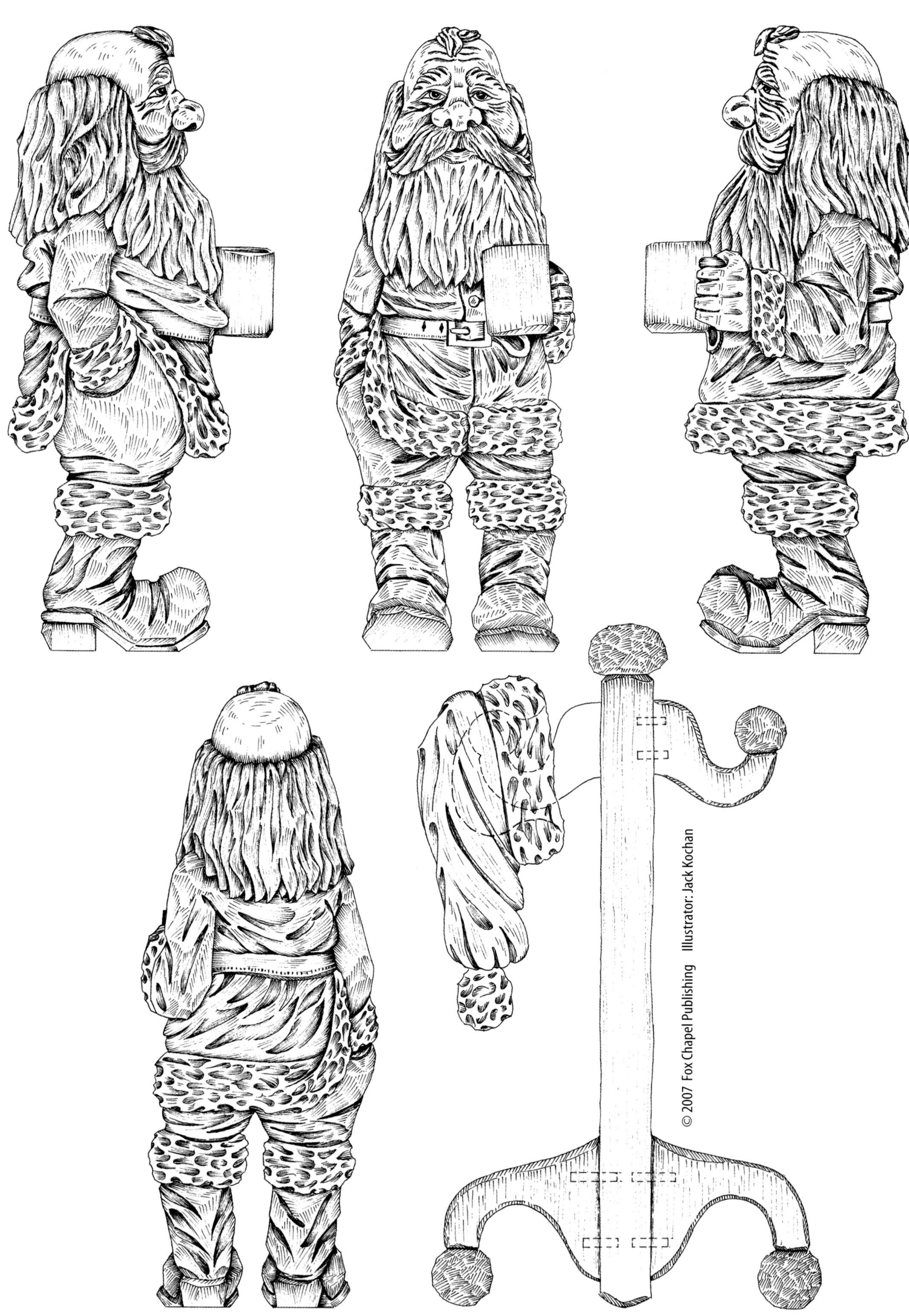
© 2007 Fox Chapel Publishing Illustrator: Jack Kochan

Santa Spiral
LENARD WATTS

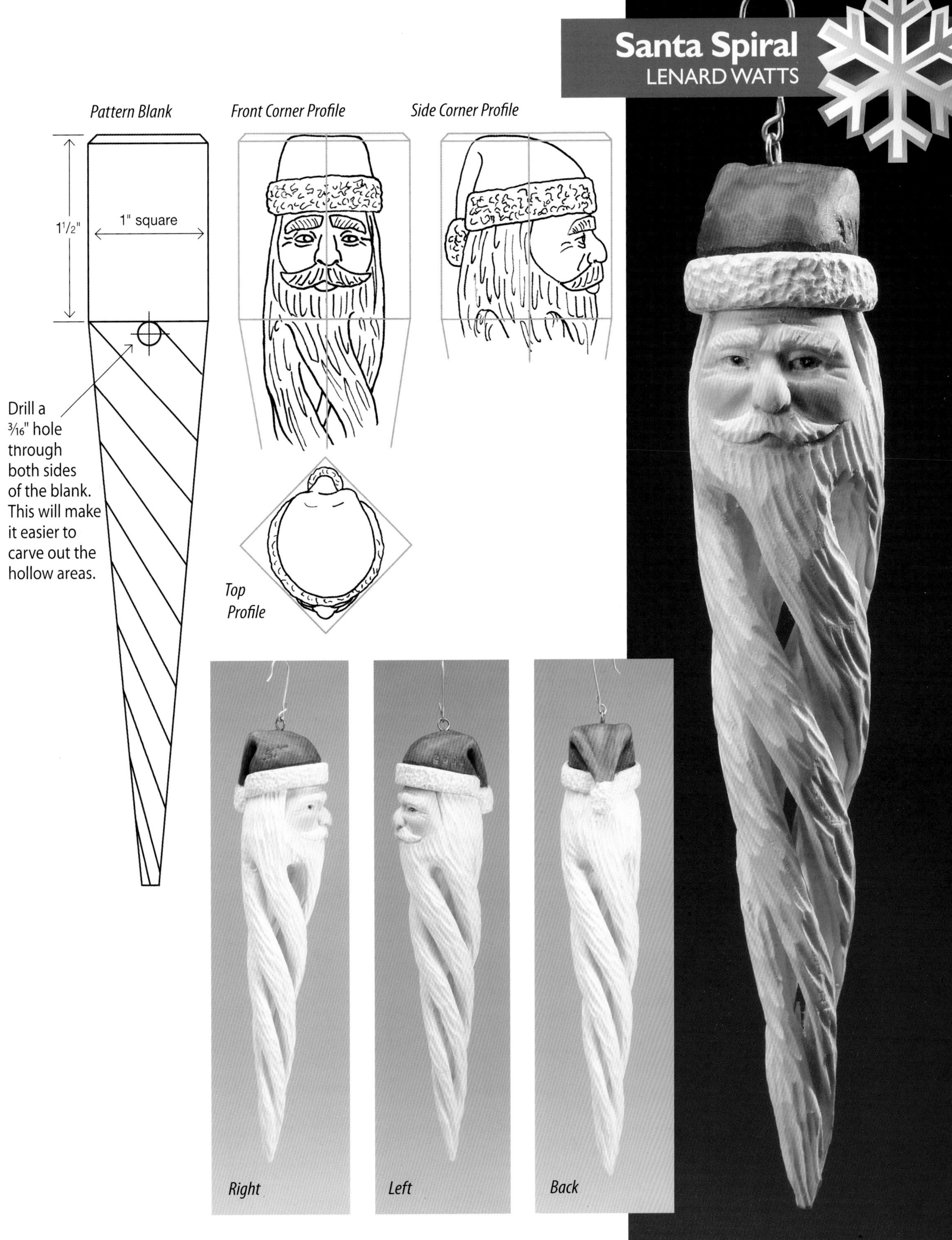

Egghead Santa

JIM FARR

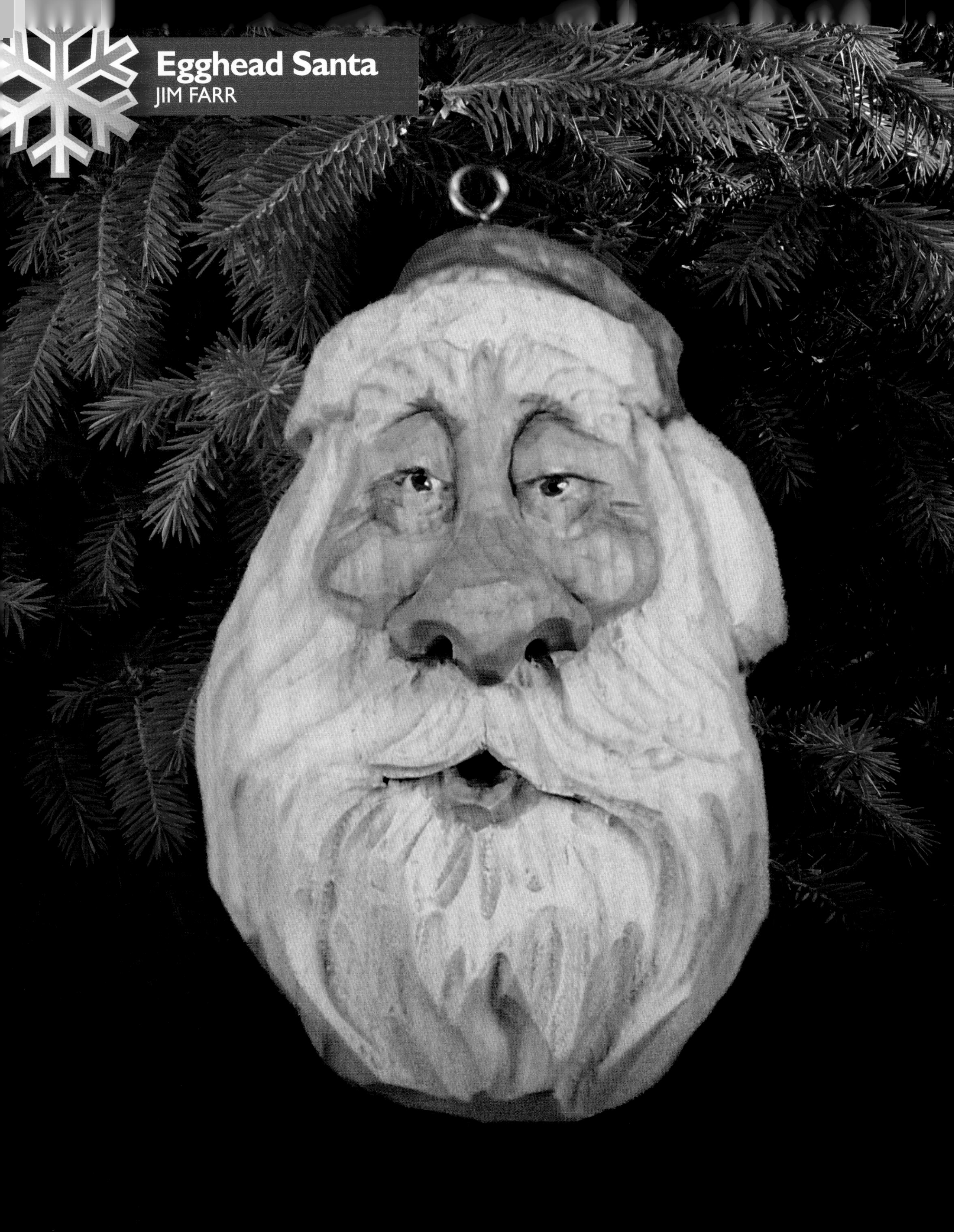

Right

Left

Back

Cowboy Santa

GERALD SEARS

Right

Front

Back

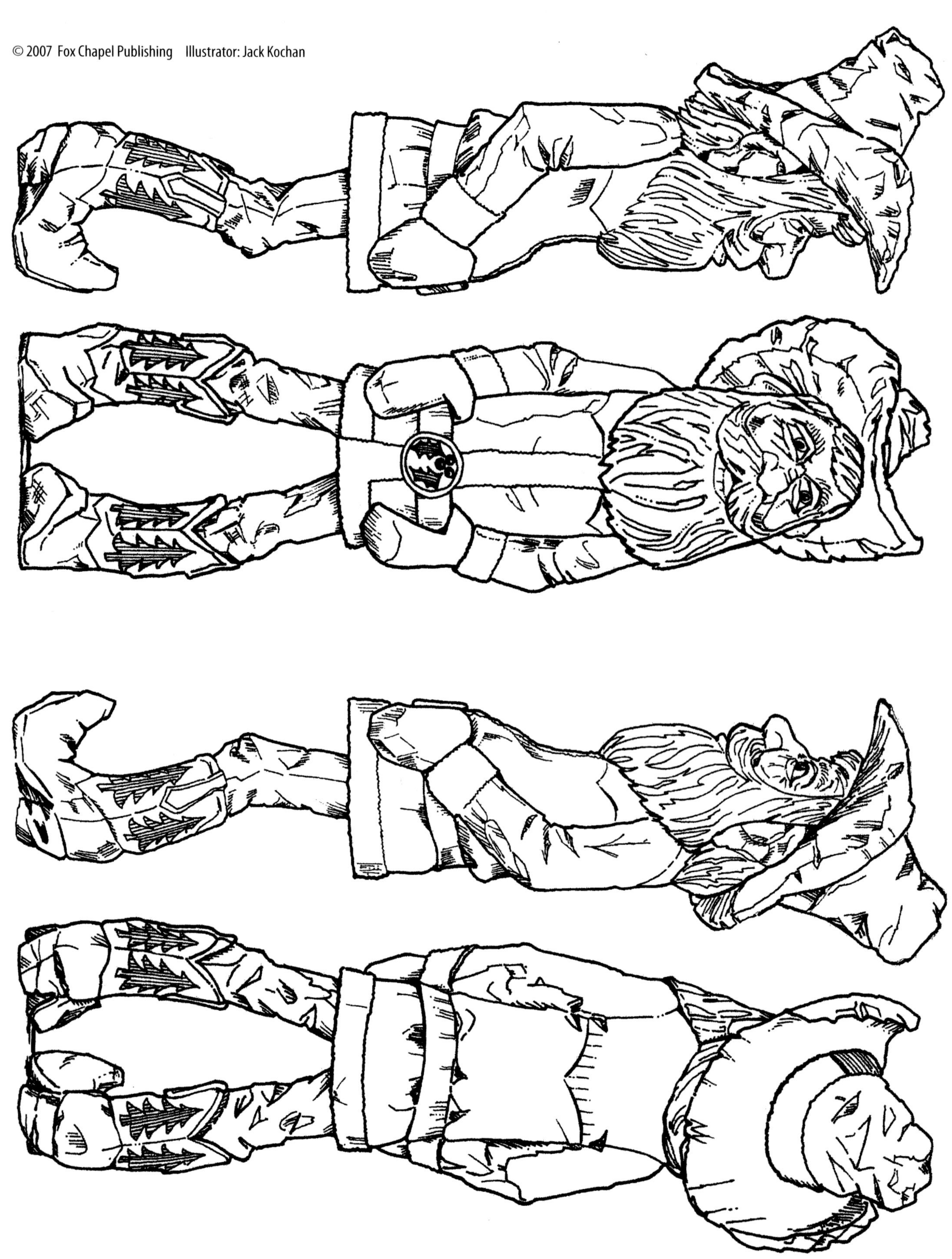

Christmas Past

JIM WILLIS

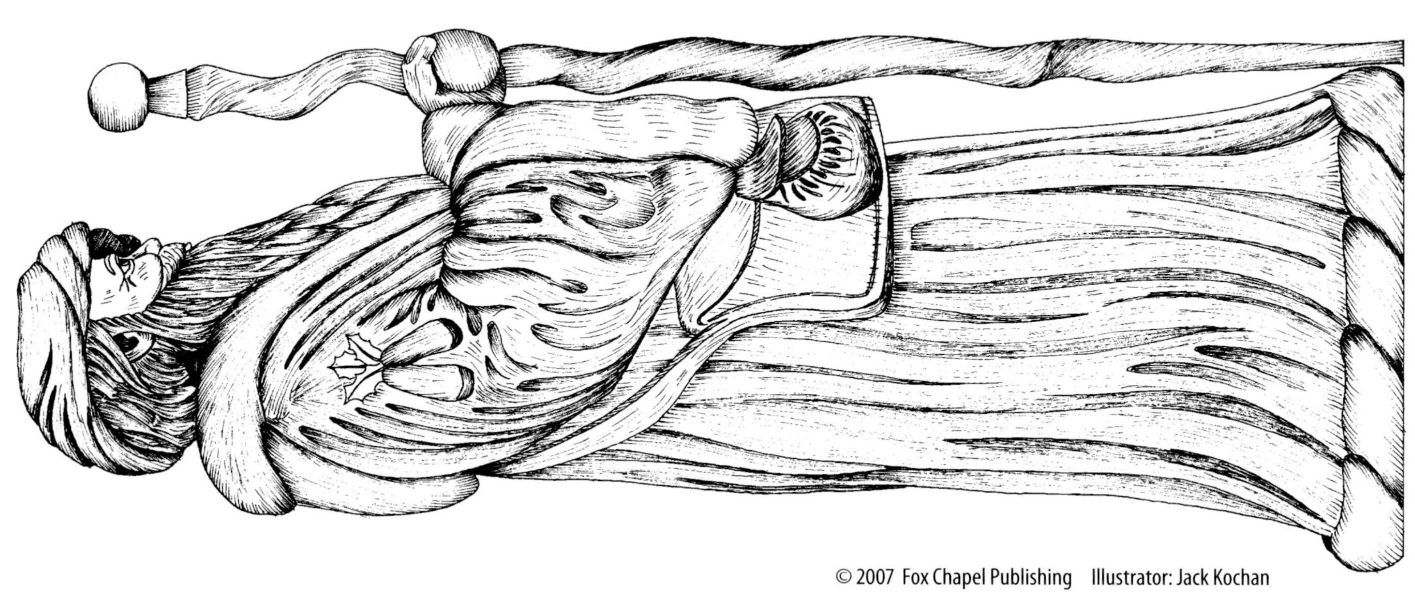

 Illustrator: Jack Kochan

Note:
Staff is carved as
a separate piece,
then cut in two
and fitted into a
hole drilled in
the mitten.

St. Nick Cane Topper

PHIL BISHOP

Right

Left

Back

 Illustrator: Jack Kochan

Tapestry Santa

TINA TONEY

Right

Front

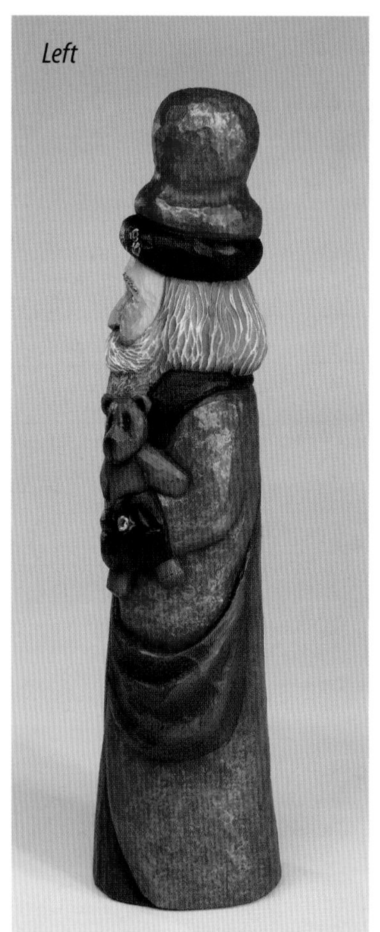
Left

Back

Santa Lamp Finial

STEVE BROWN

© 2007 Fox Chapel Publishing Illustrator: Joel Gehman

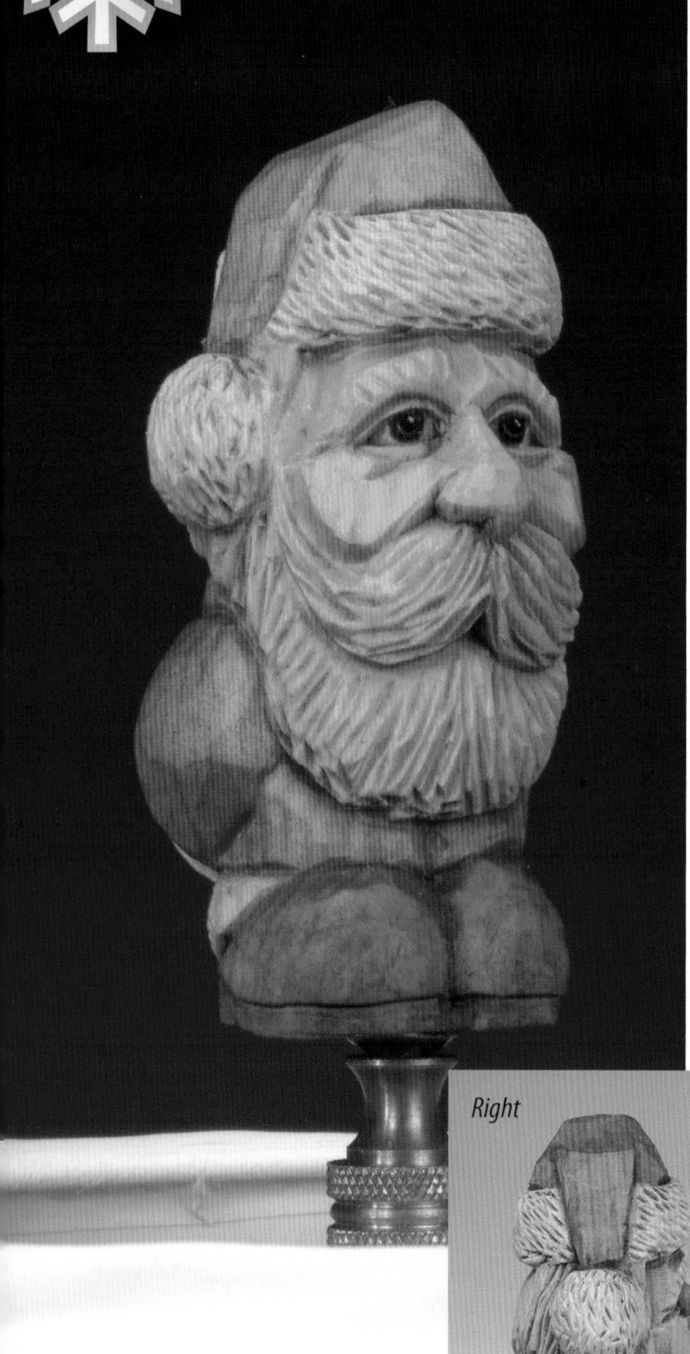

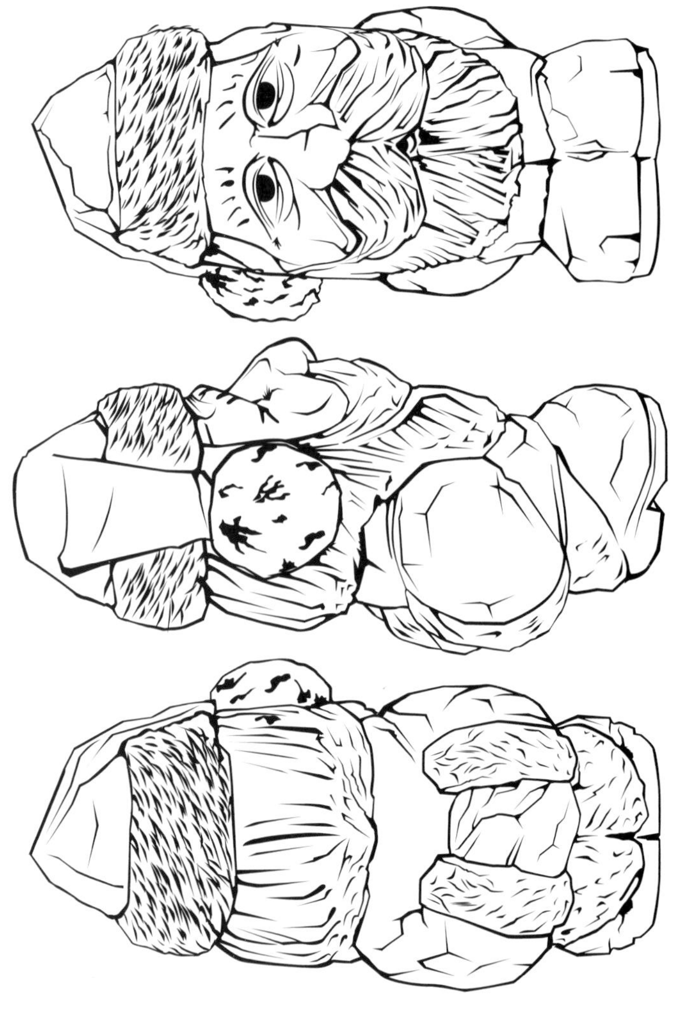

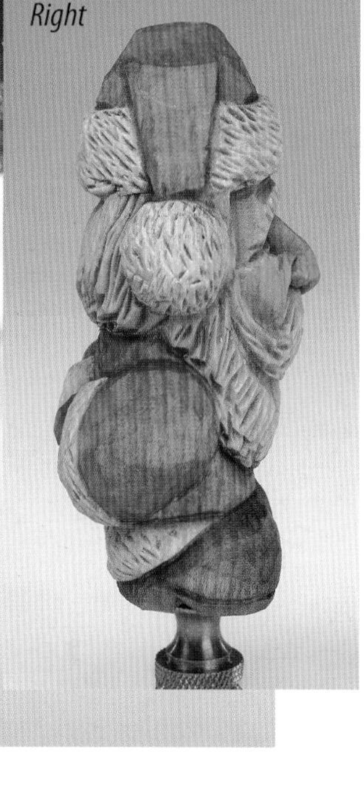

Right

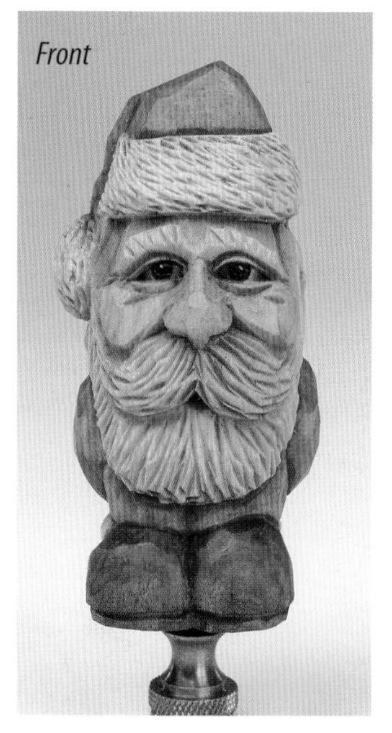

Front

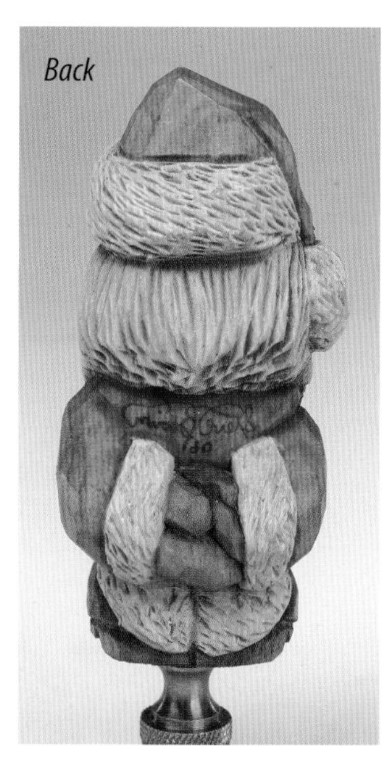

Back

Happy Santa

TINA TONEY

Right

Front

Left

Back